Ancient Egypt
and the Near East

—AN ILLUSTRATED HISTORY—

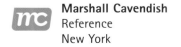 **Marshall Cavendish**
Reference
New York

Marshall Cavendish

Copyright © 2011 Marshall Cavendish Corporation

Published by Marshall Cavendish Reference
An imprint of Marshall Cavendish Corporation

Library of Congress Cataloging-in-Publication Data

Ancient Egypt and the Near East : an illustrated history.
    p. cm.
  Includes index.
  ISBN 978-0-7614-7934-5 (alk. paper)
  1. Egypt--History--To 332 B.C. 2. Middle East--History--To 622. 3. Egypt--History--To 332 B.C.--Pictorial works. 4. Middle East--History--To 622--Pictorial works. I. Marshall Cavendish Corporation.
  DT83.A6563 2011
  939'.4--dc22
                                                    2010002768

Printed in Malaysia

14 13 12 11 10   1 2 3 4 5

MARSHALL CAVENDISH
Publisher: Paul Bernabeo
Project Editor: Brian Kinsey
Production Manager: Mike Esposito

THE BROWN REFERENCE GROUP LTD
Managing Editor: Tim Harris
Designer: Lynne Lennon
Picture Researcher: Laila Torsun
Indexer: Ann Barrett
Design Manager: David Poole
Editorial Director: Lindsey Lowe

Other Marshall Cavendish Offices:

Marshall Cavendish International (Asia) Private Limited, 1 New Industrial Road, Singapore 536196 • Marshall Cavendish International (Thailand) Co Ltd. 253 Asoke, 12th Flr, Sukhumvit 21 Road, Klongtoey Nua, Wattana, Bangkok 10110, Thailand • Marshall Cavendish (Malaysia) Sdn Bhd, Times Subang, Lot 46, Subang Hi-Tech Industrial Park, Batu Tiga, 40000 Shah Alam, Selangor Darul Ehsan, Malaysia

Marshall Cavendish is a trademark of Times Publishing Limited

All websites were available and accurate when this book was sent to press.

CONTENTS

FOREWORD

I t is difficult to emphasize enough in a fore-word of 750 words the importance of study-ing the history and civilization of the cultures that are presented in *Ancient Egypt and the Near East: An Illustrated History*. More than 50 cen-turies of human history, 6000–330 BCE, are sur-veyed, and when woven together the tapestry that emerges is not only rich in detail, but mam-moth in size. Its pattern depicts kingdoms and royal dynasties that overlap, interlock, and dis-appear into each other. Amid complicated sequences of conflict and cooperation, what her-alds the advent or apogee of one culture often signals the nadir of another.

Until recent times, the origin of humanity's spiritual and intellectual achievement has been sought almost exclusively in the words of the Bible and amid the cultural remains of Greece and Italy. However, the discoveries made by archaeologists during the past 175 years have clearly demonstrated that the peoples of the ancient Near East have played crucial roles in forming our common human heritage. For it was in the ancient Near East more than 5,000 years ago that people learned to live in cities, invented effective systems of writing, and devel-oped highly evolved civilizations. It is not hard to see that an understanding of what they did so long ago gives us both a map and a key to today's political, social, and economic geography.

Faced with a massive array of influential names and places, one stumbles among them to find a vantage point and is reduced to stuttering with the staccato beat of a cultural Morse code: Luxor, Babylon, and Tyre! Ur, Nineveh, and

Jerusalem! Palmyra, Petra, and Persepolis! Akhenaton, Ramses, and Nefertiti! Sargon, Nebuchadnezzar, and Hammurabi! Cyrus, Ashurbanipal, and Sennacherib! Sustaining the endeavors of these people and their cities were famous rivers, the Nile, the Euphrates, and the Tigris, and a stream of languages from Akkadian, Arabic, Aramaic, Hebrew, and Hittite to Sumerian cuneiform and Egyptian hieroglyphics flowed along their banks.

The West has long been fascinated by the East. The former's music, art, literature, and architecture are peppered with learned and romanticized interpretations of the latter. The formal study of these cultures, languages, and peoples forms the substance of the modern aca-demic discipline known as Near Eastern Studies. We have today major centers for scholarship on both sides of the Atlantic. These include the Egyptian Museum of Antiquities, founded in Cairo in 1835, the Oriental Institute and the Sackler Library at the University of Oxford, and the Oriental Institute founded in Chicago in 1919 by Egyptologist James Henry Breasted (1865–1935). Business and philanthropic organ-izations are also contributing to the field. In November 2009, Google announced that it would provide free access to images of the arti-facts included in the collections of the Iraqi National Museum. In Syria, the World Monuments Fund and the Aga Khan Trust for Culture are working together to preserve and interpret the archaeological remains at Aleppo.

Nevertheless, advances in Near Eastern histo-riography have been hindered by the lack of any comprehensive, indigenous accounts and by the dispersal of archaeological finds to myriad public and private collections around the world. Nonetheless, from the 19th century up to the present day we have learned much and continue to do so from an astonishing array of archaeological discoveries. Assyriologist George Smith (1840–1876) thrilled the world when he discovered the *Epic of Gilgamesh* and the Chaldean account of the Great Flood while working at the British Museum among the cuneiform tablets found by Austen Layard (1817–1894). So did Howard Carter (1874–1939), a former student of the Flinders Petrie (1853–1942) who held the first chair of Egyptology in the United Kingdom, when Carter peered by candlelight into the tomb of Tutankhamen in November 1922. During the same period, major discoveries were made at Ur and Nimrud by the Mesopotamian archaeologists Charles Leonard Woolley (1880–1960) and Max Mallowan (1904–1978).

However, every journey of learning starts with an initial step, and *Ancient Egypt and the Near East: An Illustrated History* is a splendid place to begin. Students who fall captive to the intrinsic interest and sheer magnitude of the achievements here presented may find the start of a lifetime's interest or even a professional career, for much work remains to be done. In this light, we may well change the last word of a famous passage from Percy Bysshe Shelley's poem "Ozymandias" (1818) and declare: "Look on my works, ye Mighty, and *celebrate!*"

Michele Ronnick

Michele Ronnick is president of the Classical Association of the Middle West and South and a professor in the Department of Classical and Modern Languages, Literatures, and Cultures at Wayne State University, Detroit, MI.

Additional related information is available in the 11-volume *History of the Ancient and Medieval World*, second edition, and the corresponding online *Ancient and Medieval World* database at www.marshallcavendishdigital.com.

EGYPT'S OLD KINGDOM

Egypt was home to one of the world's earliest civilizations. The first major period of its history, lasting around 400 years, is known as the Old Kingdom. It was during this time that the three great pyramids were built at Giza.

The land of Egypt, which lies in the northeast corner of the African continent, is bounded to the north by the Mediterranean Sea and on all other sides by desert. If it were not for the Nile River, Egypt would be completely barren.

The Nile is the life blood of Egypt. This mighty river is one of the longest in the world. Its source is the Kagera River, which drains into Lake Victoria in east Africa, far to the south. The Nile (called the White Nile at this point) then flows north for 3,470 miles (5,583 km) through Sudan and Egypt to reach the Mediterranean Sea. At Khartoum in Sudan, it is joined by the Blue Nile, which rises in the Ethiopian highlands.

Both rivers are named for the color of their water. While the water of the White Nile is clear, the Blue Nile carries rich black sediment down from the highlands. When the river flooded in ancient times, as it did every year from spring until autumn, this rich silt was deposited over most of the land in the Nile Valley and the Nile Delta. When the waters retreated, the land remained wet enough to grow crops.

The early farmers

Farming began in the Nile Valley before 6000 BCE, and the first settled communities probably date from around 4500 BCE. These early farmers, who lived in huts made of poles and sun-dried mud bricks, grew wheat for making bread and barley for brewing beer. They also kept livestock, caught fish in the Nile, hunted wild animals, and gathered wild plants and fruits.

The early Egyptians became experts at making the most of the annual inundation of the Nile. When the flood waters receded in the autumn, crops were sown that grew readily through the warm winter and could be harvested before the next flood. The land yielded rich harvests, so surpluses could be traded or stored in case of a possible famine in the future.

As settlements became larger, a division of labor became possible. Some people became potters, while others made baskets or wove flax into linen, which was made into clothes using bone needles. Jewelers produced personal ornaments made from ivory, shell, and stone beads, while stone, and metalworkers produced tools made of flint and copper.

Upper and Lower Egypt

Although these ancient Egyptians were almost entirely self-sufficient and largely isolated from the outside world, there is

This statue depicts two goddesses flanking the king Menkaure. It was made around the time of his reign in the 25th century BCE.

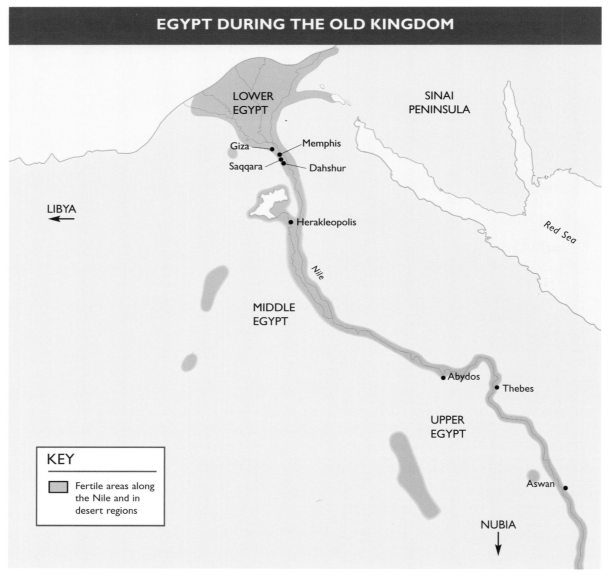

EGYPT DURING THE OLD KINGDOM

LOWER
EGYPT

SINAI
PENINSULA

Giza　Memphis

Saqqara　Dahshur

LIBYA

Red Sea

Herakleopolis

Nile

MIDDLE
EGYPT

Abydos

Thebes

UPPER
EGYPT

KEY

Fertile areas along
the Nile and in
desert regions

Aswan

NUBIA

evidence that they did have contact with other cultures. Egypt was divided geographically and culturally into two regions: the Nile Delta in the north (Lower Egypt) and the Nile Valley in the south (Upper Egypt). The inhabitants of the delta had frequent contact with neighboring people from the Mediterranean region and the Sinai Peninsula, while influences from Mesopotamia can be detected in the south. Certain types of pottery decoration

common in western Asia were adopted by the Egyptians around 3000 BCE. Also around this time, they started using cylinder seals, which were developed in Mesopotamia, to imprint on clay. The idea of pictorial writing may also have derived from Mesopotamia.

The unification of Egypt

One of the finest known examples of early hieroglyphic (pictorial) writing comes from the late Predynastic period.

Inscribed on a stone tablet, the text describes a ruler of Upper Egypt named Narmer and commemorates a series of victories over Lower Egypt. It has generally been assumed that this tablet records the unification of Egypt into one kingdom, with Narmer as its first ruler. However, later chronicles give the name of the first king of a unified Egypt as Menes. It is not clear whether Narmer and Menes are one and the same. In the early written records of Egyptian kings, Menes is listed as the first king and founder of the capital at Memphis.

The Early Dynastic period

The unification of Egypt under one king, or pharaoh, around 2925 BCE, ushered in what is called the Early Dynastic (or Archaic) period. Lasting until around 2650 BCE and covering the reigns of 12 kings, the Early Dynastic period was a time that saw many changes. The pharaohs set up huge bureaucratic systems to help administer the vast kingdom. Officials supervised the work of collecting the harvests from the farmers and distributing food to nonproductive citizens such as courtiers, priests, and civil servants. This collection and distribution process entailed keeping detailed records, so the system of writing developed rapidly at this time, together with systems of counting and measurement.

An army of scribes was kept at work busily recording state business on rolls of papyrus paper, and a rapid system of writing with pen and ink was soon in use. The advantage of writing was not only that it permitted permanent records to be kept, but that instructions and reports could be committed to papyrus rolls and sent far off by messenger.

The all-powerful kings lived in state in the capital city, Memphis. The pharaoh was considered to be a god, so his passage at death into the afterlife was supremely important. Every king commissioned his own tomb and carefully supervised the building of it. These tombs were built of sun-dried mud bricks and were designed to contain, besides the coffin of the king himself, many goods and valuable items. Sometimes, the king's wives and retainers were sacrificed at the time of his death and entombed with him. During the first dynasty, the king was buried at Abydos; during the second, he was buried at Saqqara. Around the royal burial sites were smaller tombs for members of the court.

The Old Kingdom

The third dynasty ushered in a period of high culture that was to last for five centuries. This period is now called the Old Kingdom. One of the most arresting characteristics of this period was the change in how royal tombs were built. Mud bricks were abandoned for stone blocks, and it was during this period that the great pyramids were built.

The king who initiated this change was Djoser, the second king of the third dynasty, who reigned from around 2630 to 2611 BCE. He appointed an architect, Imhotep, to build him a tomb that would be a copy of his palace, but much larger. The result was a massive stone pyramid at the center of a complex of buildings surrounded by a wall. This was the Step Pyramid (see box, page 11), which set the style for future royal tombs.

The building of the Step Pyramid and later pyramids was the spur that galvanized advancements in engineering and other skills necessary for the projects to succeed. An enormous program began to train builders and engineers, while the techniques for quarrying large blocks of stone and transporting them to the site had to be perfected. On top of this, a vast labor force was required; it is estimated that out of a population of some 1.5 million people, perhaps 70,000 workers were employed at any one time on building the pyramids. These workers

had to be supervised, fed, and sheltered during the process. Most ordinary Egyptian citizens were required to work on the pyramids, but some people were exempted. Individuals in charge of sacrificial ceremonies at temples and graves, for example, were protected under royal decree.

During the fourth dynasty, pyramid construction reached its peak. The first king of this dynasty, Snefru (ruled c. 2575–2551 BCE), built the first true pyramid at Dahshur. His son Cheops (or Khufu), who reigned from around 2551 to 2528 BCE, built the Great Pyramid of Giza, which was considered one of the great wonders of the ancient world.

Cheops's son Redjedef, who was pharaoh from around 2528 to 2520 BCE, was important in that he started to identify himself as the Son of Re (the sun god). By the beginning of the fifth dynasty, the worship of the sun god was well established.

The fifth dynasty saw the cult of the sun god grow, and several temples were built in his honor. It was also during this dynasty that the so-called Pyramid Texts first appeared. The texts were inscribed on the walls of the pyramid built for the last king of the dynasty, Unas, who reigned from around 2356 to 2325 BCE. The inscriptions were prayers and magic spells that were intended to help the dead king in the afterlife.

The divine pharaoh

In ancient Egypt, the king, or pharaoh, was an absolute ruler and was considered to be a god. He was believed to embody the creator of the world and so to be an incarnation of the god Horus. For this reason, he was often depicted as a falcon.

It was thought that the pharaoh guaranteed the fertility and prosperity of his people simply through his existence. He was also considered to be in touch with the gods and to be able to negotiate with them on behalf of his subjects. So, he was the appropriate person to make sacrifices to the gods and to offer prayers to them. However, because he could not be in every temple at one time, he appointed priests to carry out tasks on his behalf.

THE STEP PYRAMID AT SAQQARA

The Step Pyramid at Saqqara was built by the architect Imhotep at the instigation of King Djoser sometime between 2630 and 2611 BCE. The pyramid was the first large building to be made entirely of cut stone blocks, and it was far larger than anything that had gone before. The Step Pyramid paved the way for the great pyramids of the following century.

Imhotep chose a site where his building would dominate the area. There he built a six-stepped pyramid that was 200 feet (61 m) tall and symbolized the hill on which creation began. The pyramid was surrounded by other large buildings. The whole complex was bounded by a wall that was more than 1 mile (1.6 km) long.

Enclosed within the wall were buildings such as a temple and storage rooms for provisions and grave goods that had also been provided in earlier royal tombs. What was new, however, was a court where the king could celebrate his jubilees— ceremonies through which the power of the king was believed to be ritually renewed.

All the buildings were lavishly furnished and decorated. In the underground rooms, for example, the walls were hung with panels of blue-glazed tiles, while in another location, there were low-relief carvings that showed the king performing the running ceremony that was part of his coronation. A life-size statue of Djoser seated on his throne was installed in a special room close to the temple, and many other statues of gods and of members of the royal family were dotted around the enclosure. The storage rooms contained more than 40,000 stone vessels, which probably contained wine, oil, and foodstuffs.

The temple in the complex had an important role to play in the cult of dead kings. Priests in the temple carried out ceremonies and rituals that were designed to serve the dead kings in the same way as they had when the kings were alive. In this way, the present king's ancestors were venerated, and the continuity that was essential to Egyptian civilization was preserved.

The Step Pyramid of Djoser stands in the desert at Saqqara. In the foreground are stone replicas of the kiosks that would have been in use during festivals to celebrate the royal jubilee.

THE DYNASTIES

Historians divide ancient Egyptian history into dynasties. A dynasty generally means a line of hereditary rulers, and a change of dynasty would suggest that another ruling family had taken power. In the third century BCE, a writer called Manetho divided Egyptian history into 30 dynasties, many of which were based on the capital city of the ruling party.

The dates of the various dynasties have been gathered by archaeologists from tombs and ancient texts and are very approximate. The very earliest history of Egypt is called the Predynastic period and dates from around 5000 BCE to around 2925 BCE. It was followed by the Early Dynastic period (also called the Archaic period).

The approximate dates of the dynasties of the Early Dynastic period and the Old Kingdom are as follows:

THE EARLY DYNASTIC PERIOD
(c. 2925–2650 BCE)

First dynasty	c. 2925–2775 BCE
Second dynasty	c. 2775–2650 BCE

THE OLD KINGDOM
(c. 2650–2150 BCE)

Third dynasty	c. 2650–2575 BCE
Fourth dynasty	c. 2575–2465 BCE
Fifth dynasty	c. 2465–2325 BCE
Sixth dynasty	c. 2325–2150 BCE

The three great pyramids at Giza were all built during the Old Kingdom. Their construction required huge resources.

Society in the Old Kingdom

The cost of building the pyramids was astronomical. The money for them came both from the king's private resources and from taxes. The collection of taxes was one of the chief occupations of the vast bureaucracy. The most important officials were often relatives of the king; the vizier (or chief minister) was usually his son. On the other hand, *nomarchs*, the officials who governed the provinces (*nomes*), were drawn from local families.

Provincial governors could also be given other assignments. During the sixth dynasty, around 2200 BCE, the *nomarch* Harkhuf of Aswan was sent on an expedition to Nubia (present-day Sudan). Other expeditions were sent to Punt (present-day Somalia), to the Sinai Peninsula, and to Byblos, a port in present-day Lebanon.

Deceased officials were interred in *mastabas* (rectangular stone graves) surrounding the pyramids. *Mastaba* chapels were beautifully decorated with scenes from the daily life of the departed.

The achievements during the Old Kingdom were not limited to the engineering and architecture of the pyramids. The period also produced notable sculpture and painting and made significant advances in science and medicine, particularly in anatomy, surgery, and antiseptics. Astronomers made a great contribution to the science of navigation and formulated the first solar calendar with a year of 365 days.

Foreign affairs

Except for minor military expeditions conducted by Snefru into Nubia, Libya, and the Sinai Peninsula, and incursions into Asia during the fifth dynasty, Egypt had no conflict with its neighbors under the Old Kingdom and had no standing army. There was little fear of invasion; the country was protected by its natural borders of deserts to the west and east and the first cataract (rapids) of the Nile in the south. However, in the coming centuries, in the Middle and New Kingdoms, this situation would change as Egypt increasingly entered into wars with its neighbors.

The interior of the tomb of the pharaoh Unas is covered with thousands of written spells, now known as the Pyramid Texts.

See also:

Egypt's Middle Kingdom (page 14) • Egypt's New Kingdom (page 28)

EGYPT'S MIDDLE KINGDOM

A fter the anarchy of the First Intermediate period, Egypt entered into a period of relative stability, now known as the Middle Kingdom. Under rulers such as Sesostris I and Amenemhet III, Egypt became prosperous once again.

As Egypt's Old Kingdom drew to a close, the authority of the pharaoh increasingly became undermined by the provincial governors (*nomarchs*), who were building strong bases of power. During the sixth dynasty (c. 2325–2150 BCE), plots against the kings were common. Pepy I (ruled c. 2289–2255 BCE) was even threatened by a conspiracy organized by his wife. In Pepy II's reign (2246–2152 BCE), the vizier was said to have controlled the kingdom almost without reference to the pharaoh.

From the end of the sixth dynasty to the beginning of the ninth, kings followed one another in rapid succession. Egyptian king lists and the chronicle of the writer-priest Manetho suggest there were scores of kings during this era and that their combined reigns extended over a period of 150 years. However, present-day historians estimate that this period only lasted for around 20 years.

Few pyramids or other monuments were built at this time. No king reigned long enough to embark on a major construction, and the disintegration of the bureaucracy meant that the systems were no longer in place to collect the taxes necessary to fund large building projects. The pyramid built by Pepy II was the last great mortuary building of the Old Kingdom and shows a marked decline in both size and craftsmanship.

The First Intermediate period

The seventh dynasty marked the beginning of what historians call the First Intermediate period, which was a time of confusion, bordering on anarchy. The authority of the pharaoh in Memphis was weakening, and the *nomarchs* were becoming more powerful, setting up separate independent dynasties in different parts of the country.

There is evidence, too, that the climate was changing. The waters of the Nile were lower, and dust storms sweeping in from the south were covering the land with sand dunes. There was famine, and many people died of hunger. In the face of these catastrophes, it was hard for the pharaoh to retain his influence over his people; as a god-king, he was expected to interact with the gods to ensure the prosperity of his domain.

A divided kingdom

With the eighth dynasty, the domination of the Memphis kings came to an end. The effect of this change can be seen both in the architecture and the religion of ancient Egypt. The building of massive royal tombs ceased, and with the pharaoh

This pillar from the Middle Kingdom depicts Sesostris I, one of the most powerful kings to reign during the period. He built a number of great temples and monuments.

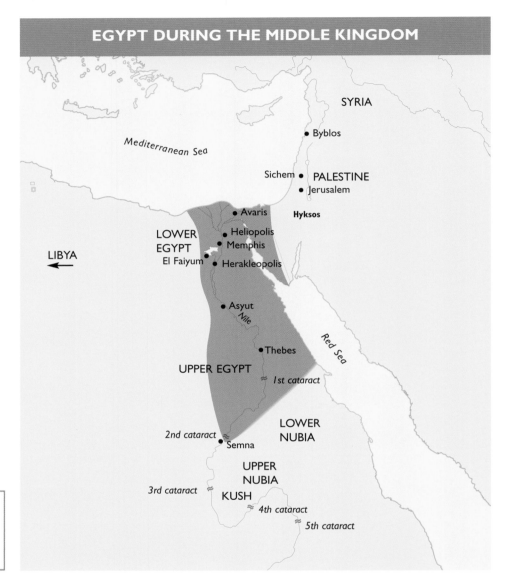

EGYPT DURING THE MIDDLE KINGDOM

SYRIA

● Byblos

Mediterranean Sea

Sichem ● PALESTINE

● Jerusalem

● Avaris **Hyksos**

LOWER
EGYPT
● Heliopolis
● Memphis

LIBYA

El Faiyum ● Herakleopolis

● Asyut

Nile

● Thebes

UPPER EGYPT

Red Sea

1st cataract

LOWER
NUBIA

2nd cataract ● Semna

UPPER
NUBIA

3rd cataract KUSH

4th cataract

5th cataract

KEY

Area of Egyptian
control during the
Middle Kingdom

no longer venerated as a supreme divine king, the rulers of the scattered feudal states that sprang up could make extravagant claims on their own tombs that they alone were responsible for the crops flourishing and their people prospering. Nevertheless, there was little real prosperity. A state of virtual civil war existed as each ruler sought to protect his territory and drive out invaders, whether from the drought-stricken deserts or from neighboring districts.

Herakleopolis

Around 2130 BCE, Akhthoes, a powerful and ruthless *nomarch* from the north of the country, founded the ninth dynasty. He belonged to an influential family based at Herakleopolis. The Herakleopolitans formed the ninth and tenth dynasties and, for a time, may have succeeded in uniting Egypt again, if only nominally. They achieved some stability by improving the irrigation systems of the region (thereby improving the harvests), by reestablishing trade with Byblos (in present-day Lebanon), and by banishing immigrants from Asia. While the Herakleopolitans held sway in the north, a rival set of kings ruled in the south. They were based in the city of Thebes (present-day Luxor).

The times were far from settled, however, and there was widespread violence, hardship, and misery. Some of this pain found expression in a new type of literature that appeared around this time. It described the feelings of pessimism that were prevalent as social upheaval caused vast changes. A sample passage from a text called *Ipuwer's Warnings* illustrates this view: "But now the noblemen are sad, and the poor are happy. Each city says: Let us expel the powerful among us. Look! The poor of the land have become rich; the possessor of things [is now] the one who has nothing."

Reunification

The *nomarchs* in the south gradually expanded their power during these troubled times and eventually established the 11th dynasty. One of them, Mentuhotep II (ruled 2061–2010 BCE), was finally able to conquer the north sometime after 2047 BCE, thereby uniting Egypt under one king again. He made Thebes his capital city.

The reunification of Egypt by Mentuhotep is commonly seen as the event that marked the beginning of the Middle Kingdom. Mentuhotep enjoyed an extraordinarily long reign of 51 years. During this time, he was largely successful in restoring peace and stability to Egypt and achieving reasonable prosperity for his people.

Before the Middle Kingdom, Thebes had been a relatively insignificant town, but with a new pharaoh in residence and with its new status as Egypt's capital city, it became the center of a huge building program. A number of great temples and monuments were erected, many of them dedicated to a particular god, Mentu, who was portrayed with a falcon's head and was associated with battle. The remains of several Middle Kingdom temples dedicated to Mentu have been discovered in the city. Other major deities were the fertility god Min, who

This wooden model that depicts bakers at work was made during the Middle Kingdom.

Mentuhotep II, depicted here in a Middle Kingdom wall painting, reunited Egypt around 2047 BCE.

of a rock tomb with a separate mortuary temple, continuing the tradition of the Old Kingdom pyramids, which had temples connected to them. Mentuhotep's tomb had no pyramid, however. The temple was dedicated both to the king and to the gods—initially Mentu and later Amon-Re. Under the temple were several tombs for Mentuhotep's wives.

Mentuhotep also built temples to the gods in other parts of Egypt. The relief decorations of all these temples show a marked return to a more artistic style, after the decline in quality during the First Intermediate period.

Mentuhotep III, Mentuhotep's son, inherited a peaceful kingdom. Civil strife was barely a memory after 50 years of stability. One major event in the reign of Mentuhotep III was a trading expedition to Punt, for which the pharaoh assembled a force of 3,000 men. He also organized a major expedition, led by his vizier Amenemhet, to Wadi Hammamat in the eastern desert. Inscriptions found on the site suggest that the purpose of the expedition was to obtain "graywacke" (a dark gray stone) for the king's sarcophagus.

Accession of Amenemhet I

Historians know little about the period that immediately followed the death of Mentuhotep III. However, after a short interlude, the throne was taken by Amenemhet I, almost certainly the vizier Amenemhet who was sent to quarry stone at Wadi Hammamat. He may have seized power by violent means. At any rate, the chronicler Manetho starts a new dynasty—the 12th—at this point.

A propagandist literary text of the period, *The Prophecy of Neferti*, suggests that, at the very least, Amenemhet's accession was unexpected. In the text,

originally came from Koptos, and the local god Amon. Amon assumed the properties of both Min and the sun god Re to become Amon-Re, the god of fertility and the father of the gods. The well-preserved ruins of a temple dedicated to him can be seen today at Karnak, a temple complex near Thebes.

Mentuhotep built his own funeral monument in the valley of Deir el-Bahri, on the west bank of the Nile opposite Thebes. The complex consisted

King Snefru of the Old Kingdom receives ominous predictions from the prophet Neferti about Egypt's future. In the prophecy, Egypt is beset by anarchy. However, a king named Ameny (a thinly disguised Amenemhet) rises from the south to restore order by force. The story was intended to legitimize Amenemhet's reign and to minimize the significance of the previous dynasty. *The Prophecy of Neferti* is an example of the way in which literature was used at this time to serve the purposes of the ruling king. In this instance, he was depicted as more accessible and more human than the godlike pharaohs of the past.

A reign of peace

Despite the fact that Amenemhet seized the throne by violent means, he enjoyed a peaceful reign. He moved his court to the north, founding a new capital just south of Memphis. There he built an impressive royal residence, which he called Itj-towy (meaning "seizing the Two Lands"). He also built himself a pyramid tomb of mud bricks in the style of the Old Kingdom. Amenemhet was determined to preserve national unity, and although the *nomarchs* continued to exercise considerable local power, he insisted that they should recognize his overall authority. He reshaped Egypt's internal administration and had a new staff of scribes educated. He reinforced the country's borders by building a "king's wall" east of the Nile Delta to prevent incursions by people from the Sinai Peninsula. He also began the construction of large fortresses along the Nile in Nubia. To the west, the desert people were repelled by means of military expeditions.

During his final years, Amenemhet ruled jointly with his son, Sesostris, to ensure a smooth succession. However, the end of Amenemhet's reign was brought about by violence; he was assassinated in a court conspiracy while Sesostris was away on a military expedition. The circumstances surrounding Amenemhet's death are similar to those described in a literary text of the period entitled *The Story of Sinuhe*. In the story, Sinuhe, who takes part in a campaign led by the crown prince Sesostris, fears that

Karnak, on the banks of the Nile near Thebes, was an important religious site in ancient Egypt.

he will be involved in court intrigue and flees to Palestine. Sinuhe is later asked to return to Egypt by the new king, Sesostris I, who succeeded in spite of the conspiracy. In another text, *The Lesson of Amenemhet*, the deceased king appears to his son in a dream and advises him to trust no one; a king has no friends, he says, only responsibilities.

Literature and history

The surviving texts from the Middle Kingdom (see box, page 24) do provide a considerable amount of historical information, while the elegant style of writing makes them absorbing works of literature as well. In place of the archaic stiffness and elaborate praise of the old tomb inscriptions, these texts are lively and occasionally even critical of society.

Many of the texts express a feeling of disillusionment, an attitude that extended to the Egyptians' view of the hereafter. Some harpists' songs called on the listeners to enjoy life on earth because only decline awaited them after death. This view is illustrated in one pessimistic story that consists of a dialogue between a man and his soul, or *ba*. The man says he is tired of life and is considering killing himself. His *ba*, which greatly prefers earthly life, threatens to leave the man if he goes through with it. This attitude is in striking contrast to the earlier Egyptian belief that life after death would be a happier continuation of life on earth.

In the Old Kingdom, the rituals of preparing a deceased person for life in the hereafter had been centered around the pharaoh. After his death, he was said to become a god, with his living and dead subjects as his dependents. It is doubtful whether the ordinary Egyptian had much hope of a life in the hereafter. However, this view changed in the course of the First Intermediate period. The ordinary Egyptian no longer depended on his king after death; he himself could obtain divine status by becoming one with Osiris, the god of death.

Life after death

In the Middle Kingdom, elaborate funeral rituals were carried out for Egypt's wealthier and more important citizens. The body was embalmed, swathed in linen, and buried in a rectangular wooden coffin. The inside of the coffin was often inscribed with magic sayings—so-called coffin texts. By providing answers to the difficult questions that would be asked, the texts would help the deceased reach the hereafter safely. This knowledge, together with impeccable behavior in life, was of major importance in obtaining life after death.

To sustain the deceased in their future lives, food was placed in the tombs, together with models of objects that would be useful, such as wooden figurines of servants, workshops, ships with their crews, and armies. Figures known

This statue from around 1700 BCE depicts a scribe called Senebtyfy. His full figure is an indication of wealth.

The gods Anubis and Ammit weigh the heart of someone who has recently died. Ammit devoured the souls of people who had not lived a virtuous life.

as *ushebtis* or *shawabtis* accompanied the deceased. *Usheb* means "answer" and *shawab* means "persea wood," so the names allude both to the function of the figures—answering the gods—and to the substance from which they were initially made.

Although the dead were provided with equipment of their own, it was expected that they would need additional food, and for this, they remained dependent upon the king. He had to appease the gods so they would receive and feed his subjects. The inscriptions on the steles (tombstones), which expressed the deceased's wish to continue to receive food, always start with the words "an offering given by the king."

The offerings were not only symbolic; the surviving next-of-kin made gifts of real food to deceased relatives, usually on holy days. The rich could also hire the services of special priests, generally connected to the local temple for this purpose. The tomb of the provincial administrator Djefai-Hapi, near Asyut, dates from the 12th dynasty and contains wall inscriptions that list a number of contracts he made with priests prior to his death. The contracts commit the priests to make offerings at his burial chapel, and the reward was to consist of the offerings themselves; after death, he, like the gods, could consume the offerings only in spirit, so the bread, beer, and meat that were offered remained for the priests after the ritual. This was a common practice.

Stability and growth

The 12th dynasty lasted from 1991 to 1783 BCE. For two centuries, Egypt experienced major political and economic growth. Stability was achieved by

LIFE IN ANCIENT EGYPT

The majority of the Egyptian people were peasants who farmed the narrow areas of land bordering the Nile River. Their lives were dominated by the annual flooding of the river, which brought water to a parched land and rendered it fertile by depositing a rich layer of silt. The flood determined the cycle of plowing, sowing, and harvesting. The major crops were wheat and barley, which were used to make bread and beer, and flax, which was used to make linen. In the oases and other irrigated areas, the horticultural products included grapes, dates, and figs. Meat was supplied by cattle and poultry and, to a lesser extent, by pigs, goats, and desert animals.

These peasant farmers lived in small villages of mud huts near the land they worked, and most of the labor involved in raising crops was to do with keeping them watered, by digging or cleaning out water channels or by carrying water from the river in pots slung on a yoke. When time for the harvest came around, the tax collector also appeared—to take his due of the crops to feed the nonproductive members of the population.

In the highly evolved Egyptian society of that time, nonproductive people were legion. Apart from ordinary craftsmen who produced baskets, pots, and wooden utensils, there were butchers, ropemakers, weavers, and brewers. Stonemasons were needed to build the temples and monuments, and jewelers were needed to produce the intricate jewelry and ornaments required for royal tombs. In addition, there was an army of civil servants to administer the state, plus scribes and priests.

Society was strictly regulated, and settlements were established by the government for artisans, civil servants, and temple personnel. These people were provided with small houses and wages in kind—usually food rations. Egyptian society also had many slaves, who were often prisoners of war. Many slaves worked on the pyramids, temples, and palaces, but some were owned by private individuals.

According to the letters of Hekanakhte from the time of Mentuhotep II, there was ample opportunity for well-to-do Egyptians to acquire and add to private holdings of land. It is clear that Hekanakhte himself owned or leased several plots of land that were cultivated by his sons and servants. With the proceeds, he was able to support his extensive household. However, the letters reveal that his relatives complained about the small portions.

Made during the Middle Kingdom, this wooden model depicts a servant girl carrying loaves of bread.

pharaohs following the example of Amenemhet I. Each of his successors ruled jointly with his respective crown prince for the last few years of his reign.

Growth and expansion

Sesostris I, the son of Amenemhet I, reigned from 1962 to 1926 BCE, consolidating and building on the achievements of his father. Sesostris initiated a great building program, constructing a new temple at Heliopolis together with many other temples and monuments all over Egypt. He built forts in Nubia (to the south), established commercial ties with Palestine and Syria (to the north), and led a campaign against the Libyans (to the west). His excursions into neighboring territories, particularly Nubia, were made for economic reasons. Nubia was rich in gold deposits, but valuable materials were also sought elsewhere. In the eastern desert, inscriptions tell of large-scale expeditions to mine high-grade stone for the construction of monuments. These expeditions involved thousands of people and animals.

Within Egypt itself, arable land was the most valuable resource. After the reign of Amenemhet II, Sesostris II, who ruled from 1897 to 1878 BCE, reclaimed land in El Faiyum (the Faiyum oasis) to the west of the Nile Valley. Evidence of this outstanding achievement was discovered by archaeologists who found the remains of the wooden floodgates that he built.

Sesostris III, who held power from 1878 to 1843 BCE, succeeded in creating a passageway through the first rocky cataract of the Nile, making it possible to travel past it for the first time. He was also a successful conqueror,

extending Egyptian rule to Semna, just south of the second cataract of the Nile. The king constructed an extensive line of fortresses to guard the second cataract and prevent Nubians and Kushites from entering Egyptian territory unless they could prove they were traders. Sesostris formed a standing army to campaign against the Nubians and built new forts on the southern frontier. His troops also penetrated far into Palestine, reaching the cities of Jerusalem and Sichem.

Administrative reforms

Sesostris was also a political reformer. For administrative purposes, he divided Egypt into four geographical units. Each was controlled by a powerful official, himself under the control of the vizier. Sesostris put an end to the independence—and the threat to his own power—of the *nomarchs* by driving them from office. From then on, the court, located in Memphis, was represented throughout Egypt by a tightly controlled system of royal supervisors. Sesostris's successor, Amenemhet III (ruled 1843–1797 BCE), continued to employ this administrative system. He also

*This **shawabti** figure has been placed in a model coffin. Such figures were expected to serve the dead in the afterlife.*

LITERATURE, LANGUAGE, AND WRITING

Old Egyptian was the written form of the language used in Egypt from the Predynastic period through to the end of the Old Kingdom, that is, from before 3000 to around 2200 BCE. It was gradually replaced during the Middle Kingdom by Middle Egyptian, a classical form of the language that was used in literature. Spoken Egyptian also changed over time, becoming increasingly remote from the literary language. Middle Egyptian, which was used from around 2200 to 1600 BCE, continued solely in written form until around 500 BCE.

The overriding tone of Middle Kingdom literature is one of disillusionment with established traditions, possibly the result of the chaotic conditions of the First Intermediate period. Many of the surviving works have a clearly political slant, including *The Prophecy of Neferti* and *The Story of Sinuhe*, which are concerned with the royal house. Many stories contain a justification or glorification of the king's behavior.

These literary texts were written on papyrus, a kind of paper made from lengths of pith cut from papyrus reeds. The pith was arranged crisscross in layers, soaked in water, pressed flat with a piece of ivory or shell, and dried. The dried rolls of papyrus were inscribed in ink with abbreviated forms of hieroglyphs.

The Greek word *hieroglyph* means "sacred carving," which reflects the original use of this pictorial script on stone monuments. There are two main forms of Egyptian hieroglyphs. The first, the hieratic (or "priestly") script, so named by the Greeks because of its original use in religious texts, was widely used from the time of the Old Kingdom. Around 650 BCE, the second form, the demotic (or "popular") script, began to replace hieratic. Demotic writing was used until around 450 CE. Egyptians believed that their script, in which only consonants were represented, had been taught to them by Thoth, the god of science and writing, and they called it "the words of the gods."

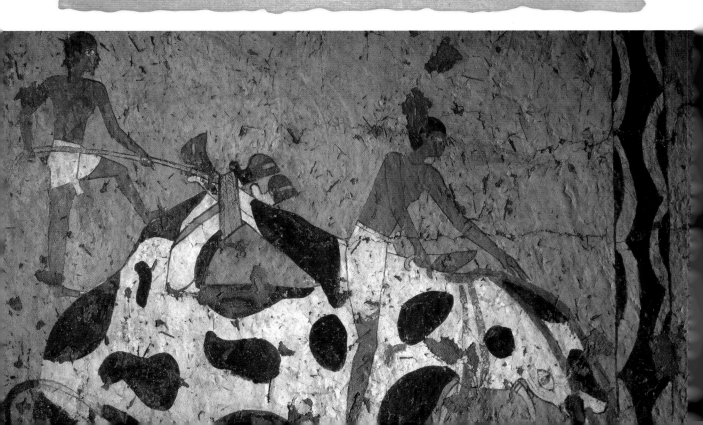

continued with Sesostris II's program of land reclamation.

During the 13th dynasty (which lasted from around 1750 to 1630 BCE), Egypt was led by 70 different pharaohs. The number of rulers suggests there may have been rival claimants to the throne at some periods and that some kings may have reigned for only a few months. The kings all claimed to rule over the whole of Egypt, and for most of the period, Itj-towy remained the royal residence. However, royal power was weakening.

North and south

Toward the end of the 13th dynasty, some of the Egyptian kings appear to have moved the seat of power to Thebes. At the same time, a rival dynasty, the 14th, became established in the Nile Delta in the north.

In addition to these internal threats to stability, Egypt was under pressure on its borders. In western Asia, tribal migration had been going on for some time—caused in part by the arrival in the area of new people from the Caucasus. The new arrivals drove many of the Semitic people living in coastal Phoenicia, Levant, and the Sinai Peninsula out into the northeastern Nile Delta. As early as the 12th dynasty, Egyptian texts refer to people called Asiatics with Semitic names. Several pharaohs of the 13th dynasty bore non-Egyptian names such as Chenger and Aya, indicating foreign origins. The fact that these foreigners could set up settlements in Egypt without being repelled suggests a weakening of the Egyptian administration.

In the south, Egypt was losing its grip on the forts built to repel the Nubians. In the east, warlike Medjay tribesmen from

This tomb painting from the First Intermediate period depicts farmers slaughtering an ox. Cattle were a source of both labor and food.

This statue depicts Sesostris III, a warrior king who expanded Egyptian control into Nubia in the 19th century BCE.

the desert infiltrated the Nile Valley and left behind evidence of their culture in the form of shallow graves filled with black-topped pottery.

At the same time that foreigners were being assimilated into Egyptian society, non-Egyptian kingdoms from western Asia were being set up in the Nile Delta. The Egyptians called these new rulers *Hekau-chasut* (desert kings). This word

This statue, made around 1800 BCE, depicts the pharaoh Amenemhet III, who ruled Egypt for more than 50 years.

appears in the writings of historians from the Greek period as "Hyksos." These kings established a dynasty (the 15th) with a capital at Avaris in the eastern delta and dominated central and northern Egypt, rivaling the weaker contemporaneous 16th dynasty.

The Second Intermediate period

The era that followed the Middle Kingdom was the Second Intermediate period. It covered the rule of the 15th dynasty (that of the Hyksos), which lasted from around 1630 to 1550 BCE, as well as the Thebes-based 16th and 17th dynasties, which lasted from around 1630

THE HYKSOS EFFECT

The takeover of Lower Egypt by the Hyksos in the 17th century BCE had many beneficial effects for Egyptian culture and technology. Until that time, Egypt's technology had lagged behind that of western Asia. However, when the Hyksos imported the technique of working with bronze, it largely replaced copper for weapons and other hardware. In warfare, the Hyksos introduced many weapons that were unknown to the Egyptians, such as the composite bow and new types of scimitars and swords. Still, the most amazing innovation, as far as the Egyptians were concerned, was the horse-drawn chariot.

On the domestic side, the Hyksos introduced an upright loom, which made weaving much easier, and an improved potter's wheel. For agriculture, they imported humpbacked bulls, olive and pomegranate trees, and new vegetable crops. For recreation, the Hyksos brought with them new musical instruments— the oboe, the tambourine, the lyre, and the long-necked lute—which were used to accompany both singing and new types of dances.

Canaanite gods such as Baal and Astarte also started to appear in Egyptian decorative motifs following the incursion of the Hyksos.

to 1550 BCE. In the north (Lower Egypt), the Hyksos kings were recognized as legitimate sovereigns. They adopted many of the existing Egyptian customs, while introducing their own culture and technology. They adopted Egyptian titles and traditions and worshipped the god Re of Heliopolis. In the south (Upper Egypt), princes based at Thebes claimed sovereignty but had to pay tribute to their Hyksos overlords.

It is possible to relate this period in Egyptian history to the time of the patriarchs of the Bible. According to the book of Genesis, Jacob settled in Egypt and his son Joseph became the vizier of the pharaoh. These stories could very well be a reference to the settling of northern Egypt by the Hyksos, who came from the same geographical region as the Israelites.

Origins of the New Kingdom

The many Egyptian kings of the 17th dynasty, all based at Thebes, tried to maintain their power over Upper Egypt, but they were squeezed between the Hyksos in the north and the kingdom of Kush in the south. Eventually, the Theban kings took up arms against their rivals. Around 1554 BCE, the Theban king Seqenenre attacked his Hyksos equivalent, Apophis. Seqenenre was unsuccessful, probably dying in battle, but the struggle was continued by his successors, Kamose (ruled 1554–1550 BCE) and Ahmose (ruled 1550–1525 BCE). Ahmose succeeded in reunifying Egypt, beginning the period known as the New Kingdom.

See also:

Egypt's New Kingdom (page 28) • Egypt's Old Kingdom (page 6)

This model depicts an ancient Egyptian sailing boat. A canopy protects its wealthy owner from the sun.

EGYPT'S NEW KINGDOM

The New Kingdom was the period in which Egypt's empire reached its greatest extent. Under warlike kings such as Thutmose I, the empire was expanded into western Asia in the north and deep into Kush in the south.

At the time of the 16th and 17th dynasties (c. 1630–1550 BCE), the Theban kings ruled over the territory between Elephantine (an island near the first cataract) and Abydos. In the north, the Hyksos held sway, with their seat of government at Avaris in the eastern delta. Toward the end of the 17th dynasty, the Theban kings began a campaign to oust the Hyksos from Egypt.

The campaign was initiated by Seqenenre (ruled 1558–1554 BCE), who launched a war against the Hyksos from his base in Thebes. However, he was not successful and probably died in battle; his mummy shows that his skull was shattered, indicating that he met a violent end. His son Kamose (ruled 1554–1550 BCE) continued the campaign. According to his stele, Kamose sailed down the Nile and succeeded in taking a Hyksos stronghold near Hermopolis.

Kamose became such a threat to the Hyksos that their king Apophis attempted to form an alliance with the king of Kush (in present-day Sudan). If Kush would attack the Thebans from the south, Kamose would be forced to fight on two fronts at once. However, while the Hyksos messenger was traveling through the desert to make the proposal to the Kushites, he was taken prisoner by Kamose's soldiers, so it is probable that the alliance never took place.

Kamose succeeded in driving the Hyksos back to the walls of Avaris but died before the city fell. After a long siege, the city was finally taken by Kamose's successor Ahmose, who thus became the pharaoh of a united Egypt.

The New Kingdom

Ahmose I was to reign over a unified Egypt for a quarter of a century. His reign marked the beginning of a period of enormous prosperity and imperial expansion, and it was during this era that the power of ancient Egypt was at its greatest. Historians call this period the New Kingdom. Ahmose also founded a new dynasty, the 18th (1550–1307 BCE), which was to include such rulers as Hatshepsut (the only woman pharaoh), Thutmose III, Akhenaton, and Tutankhamen. This period is particularly noted for the great military achievements of its pharaohs, but it is also renowned for its art, which became less bound by tradition and more open to influences from the Asiatic and Aegean civilizations.

After ousting the Hyksos from Egypt, Ahmose I pursued them into Palestine,

This wall painting of the falcon-headed god Horus is found in a tomb in the Valley of the Kings, the burial site of many New Kingdom pharaohs.

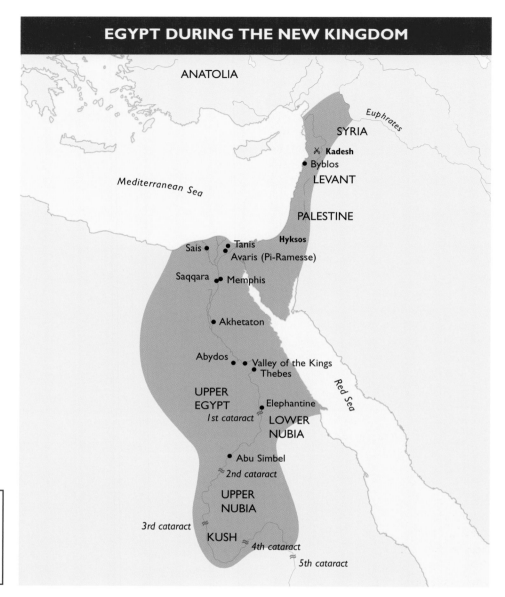

EGYPT DURING THE NEW KINGDOM

KEY

Egypt at height of the New Kingdom

✕ Major battle

establishing a base for an Egyptian presence in western Asia. The region was of vital importance because of the copper mines located there—as one of the two key ingredients of the alloy bronze, copper was a valuable metal. Ahmose then turned his attention to the southern borders of Egypt, where he subjugated the kingdom of Kush. For these campaigns, he recruited a standing army. His soldiers were well paid and were often rewarded with the spoils of battle, both loot and prisoners. They also received grants of land, which eventually gave rise to an important military class.

Ahmose ran his new empire as a military state. His administration was based on that of the Middle Kingdom, with a vizier as the head administrator. Many officials were appointed by the king from among the army officers who had campaigned with him.

The elevation of Amon

One day, according to a temple inscription, Ahmose, who had just passed through Thebes, was forced to return because of a sudden storm. He believed that the storm was caused by the god Amon showing dissatisfaction with his residence, which had seen hardly any changes in a long time. To appease the god, Ahmose started a building program, restoring and enlarging Amon's temples in Thebes, which became the empire's capital city once more.

The king, who was considered to be the son of Amon, elevated his god-father to the position of principal deity of the dynasty. In this new religious concept, the queen also had a special place. She was no longer considered to be just the king's wife, but also the wife of Amon. The Egyptians believed that, in a mystical marriage, she conceived a son by Amon. As a child of both Amon and the king, the boy was both a god and the rightful heir to the throne. This concept reinforced the continuation of the dynasty on a religious level.

Ahmose's son and successor was Amenhotep I, who acted as co-regent with his father for five years before becoming pharaoh in 1525 BCE. Amenhotep extended the empire's boundary to the south as far as the third cataract and introduced the office of "King's Son of Kush" to govern the newly colonized region. He also campaigned in Syria and expanded Egypt's borders in the Levant.

The Valley of the Kings

Because Thebes was the center of a great empire, it also became the place where its kings were buried. Although many Old Kingdom pharaohs had been buried in pyramids, it was becoming more usual by the 17th dynasty for pharaohs to be buried in tombs in the mountains on the western shore of the Nile.

The tomb chambers were hewn out of the rock and typically had an accompanying sacrificial chapel with a miniature pyramid called a pyramidion. The king was laid to rest in the rock chamber in a wooden mummy case shaped like a man. Amenhotep I departed from this custom and built his temple near the river bank.

This black granite statue is believed to depict the pharaoh Thutmose I, who greatly expanded the borders of Egypt's empire.

Amenhotep's tomb has not been located with certainty; he was the first king to hide his burial place by placing it somewhere apart from his mortuary temple. This action started a new custom, but the kings who came after Amenhotep had their tombs built in the Valley of the Kings.

This valley is hidden by high cliffs and can be approached only through a narrow passageway. It may be that the move to locate tombs in the valley was an attempt to foil grave robberies, which were already prevalent. The first pharaoh to be buried in the valley was Amenhotep's successor, Thutmose I. The entrance to his tomb, like that of the other tombs in the valley, was hidden after it was sealed.

More than 60 tombs have been found at this site, most of them having several rooms carved out of solid rock. The first tomb to be discovered was found empty in 1817 CE and belonged to Seti I. Seti's body was discovered along with the reburied mummies of 39 other pharaohs in a single vault in 1881 CE. The bodies of their wives (apart from Hatshepsut, queen of Thutmose II and a ruler herself) were found buried a few miles outside the valley.

The mummification process

The pharaohs were embalmed before they were buried. This preservation of the body by embalming seems to have been practiced by the Egyptians for around 30 centuries. The process was evidently considered to be a way of allowing the body to remain united with the soul after death.

Mummies were prepared in a sophisticated procedure. First, the brain and internal organs of the dead pharaoh were removed. The body was then dehydrated with a salt called natron, a process that lasted for 40 days. The body cavity was then packed with fragrant herbs and sawdust, after which it was treated with resin and tightly wrapped in bands of linen.

The Valley of the Kings was the major burial site for Egyptian kings during the New Kingdom.

A priest wearing a mask with the features of the god Anubis bends over a mummy to perform a pre-burial ritual. This painting dates to around 1200 BCE.

SERVANTS IN THE PLACE OF TRUTH

Texts discovered near the Valley of the Kings contain an account of the lives of the workers who built the tombs in the valley. The workers were housed in a village nearby, and some of those houses are still recognizable in the present-day village of Deir el-Medina. The workers were called "Servants in the Place of Truth," and from the limestone tablets and fragments of papyrus that were discovered at Deir el-Medina, it is possible to construct a vivid picture of the workers' lives.

The documents contain reports, letters, lists of absentees, contracts, invoices, wills, and other administrative records, as well as educational, literary, and magical texts. The documents describe a privileged group of artisans who were engaged in building and decorating royal tombs on a full-time basis. Their wages were paid by the government in the form of rations, and their managers were directly accountable to the vizier, who visited the valley to inspect their work at regular intervals.

The texts also reveal a good deal about the local economy and the trading, borrowing, and lending that took place among the villagers. All goods had fixed prices, expressed in quantities of grain or silver, but were actually paid for in kind. Any dispute about a transaction could be submitted to the local council, where judgment was pronounced by a group of important villagers. There is also a record of the earliest known strikes in history. When there were delays in the distribution of rations during and after the reign of Ramses III, the workers put down their tools and marched in protest to show their displeasure and their hunger.

This wall painting from the time of the 18th dynasty depicts a scribe hunting gazelles from a chariot.

The rule of Hatshepsut

Six years into the reign of Thutmose III, Hatshepsut arranged to have herself proclaimed pharaoh. According to one version of the story, she saw the statue of Amon move toward her during a procession and took that as a sign that he had selected her to rule. Thutmose II had earlier claimed to be selected by a similar process when he was not the only candidate for the throne.

Because, according to tradition, a woman could not succeed to the throne, Hatshepsut and Thutmose III reigned jointly. Their names are both inscribed in a cartouche, an oval frame in which the names of Egyptian kings were recorded, but it is clear that Hatshepsut played the dominant role.

Even though the Hyksos had been expelled from the realm more than half a century earlier, Hatshepsut claimed that it was only her rule that had put an end to the chaos of the Hyksos era. In order to celebrate this achievement, Hatshepsut embarked on a great building program to glorify her reign, including obelisks in Karnak and a magnificent funerary temple in Deir el-Bahri.

Expanding the empire

The successor to Amenhotep I was Thutmose I, who was no relation to the former pharaoh but had been a general in his army. Thutmose (ruled c. 1504–1492 BCE) was a warrior-king who extended Egypt's borders. He occupied and subdued the whole of the Levant, establishing his furthest frontier on the Euphrates River. In the south, he conquered Upper Nubia and occupied Kush as far south as the fourth cataract. By the end of his reign, the New Kingdom had reached its greatest extent. Egypt's new territories made a huge contribution to its enormous wealth.

In 1492 BCE, Thutmose II succeeded his father. Because he was only the son of a minor wife, Thutmose married his half sister Hatshepsut to consolidate his claim to the throne. On Thutmose's death, around 1479 BCE, Thutmose III, who was still a child, ascended the throne. He ruled the country nominally, while his stepmother Hatshepsut acted as regent.

Foreign affairs

In the reliefs and the statues of her, Hatshepsut is depicted as a man, to comply with the traditional concept of the ruler being male. She is sometimes shown as an army commander, though it is doubtful that any campaigns were waged during her reign. She did, however, organize expeditions abroad, including a voyage to the African country of Punt (present-day Somalia). Reliefs in her funerary temple show pictures of the trip—the wife of a local king, houses built on stilts, and the returning ships laden with the spoils of the trip, including incense, myrrh, and exotic objects.

After Hatshepsut's death in 1458 BCE, Thutmose III became the sole monarch. Perhaps angry at the way his stepmother had kept him in the background, he had her name and image obliterated from a number of prominent monuments.

During Hatshepsut's reign, the whole of the Near East had been in turmoil. The migrations that had brought the Hyksos to Egypt had also fostered the development of new kingdoms in northern Mesopotamia, particularly those of the Mitanni. The stability of Egyptian rule was threatened by these new kingdoms and by powerful Syrian princes. Thutmose launched a series of campaigns to protect his Asian lands, successfully consolidating his position in the Levant and Syria. His expeditions are portrayed on the temple walls at Karnak.

When Thutmose was unable to subdue the Mitanni, however, he formed an alliance with them. This alliance was later reinforced by marriage through several generations; Thutmose and his successors, Amenhotep II, Thutmose IV, and Amenhotep III, all took Mitanni princesses as brides.

Both Amenhotep II (ruled 1427–1401 BCE) and Thutmose IV (ruled 1401–1391 BCE) maintained the empire by using diplomatic and military means. They succeeded in maintaining a balance of power with their neighbors, but two new kingdoms were on the rise—those of the Assyrians and the Hittites.

New Kingdom society

At the apex of Egyptian society was the pharaoh. He was both the political and religious leader. As such, he remained aloof from his people. He was believed to be in contact with the gods, which was said to guarantee the country's prosperity. The pharaoh was the guardian of mankind, the lawmaker and military commander, and he maintained order on earth and throughout the universe. As long as that order—called *ma'at* in Egyptian—was not disrupted in any way, the world would continue to exist.

The pharaoh made laws and issued decrees after consultation with his officials. However, in practice, much of the responsibility for legislation rested on his highest administrators, especially the vizier. The office of vizier carried an enormous administrative burden. In the tomb of Rekhmire, who was vizier under Hatshepsut and Thutmose III, an extensive job description of that office has been preserved. It is referred to as a "bitter task." The long enumeration of his duties shows that the vizier was responsible for maintaining order in the royal court and for controlling taxation, the royal treasuries, and the grain silos. He was also required to supervise the lower administrators and, if necessary, to punish them for failure to perform their duties.

The majority of the population worked in agriculture, which was the basis of the Egyptian economy. There were many other occupations and professions, however. There were large groups of civil servants, priests, craftsmen, and army officers. Because of the regular military campaigns of the New Kingdom, it was necessary to keep a standing army ready for action. Within the army, there were two main ranks, those of infantryman and charioteer. The

This cosmetic spoon, made around the time of the 18th and 19th dynasties, depicts a young woman carrying an amphora.

Created around 1350 BCE, this relief depicts the pharaoh Akhenaton making an offering to the sun god Aton. During Akhenaton's reign, the worship of Aton replaced that of all other gods.

commander-in-chief was the pharaoh. In preparation for this role, young princes were taught how to manage horses, chariots, and weapons from an early age.

Priests and temples

It was one of the duties of the pharaoh to appease the gods regularly by offering sacrifices in the temples. It was also his duty to build and expand the temples of the gods. The classical form of the Egyptian temple, which was the style of the New Kingdom, was designed to allow for continuous expansion. The main plan of a temple was one of halls and open courts surrounded by impressive colonnades. At its core was the sanctum, where the image of the god resided and was cared for by the priests, acting as representatives of the king. Only the highest priests were allowed to enter this most sacred part of the temple. Major temples, such as those at Karnak and Luxor, would be enlarged by adding new halls or courts to the existing ones, all forming a straight line from the sanctum to the pylon (the temple gate).

The cost of the upkeep of the temples was considerable. Substantial resources were needed to pay for the requisite religious sacrifices, to feed the temple employees (who included civil servants and workmen as well as priests), and to maintain the sanctuary itself. The pharaoh supplied these resources in the form of arable land, grassland, and cattle. In addition to this basic income, the temple would receive regular gifts of valuable objects that the king brought back from his campaigns or trading expeditions. The wars of Thutmose III, for example, contributed hundreds of pounds of gold and silver to the temple of Amon in Thebes.

The priests serving in the temples were all sons of important and influential families. To be a priest was, for the most part, an honorary position that could be held by officials in addition to their normal administrative duties, providing them with an extra source of income. The office of priest, together with its salary, was usually passed on from father to son. It was important for the king to cultivate the goodwill of the families of priests and high-ranking officials. By his careful attendance to the temples, the pharaoh both placated the gods and secured a loyal staff of civil servants throughout the country.

The Amarna period

During the reign of Amenhotep III (ruled 1391–1353 BCE), Egypt reached the peak of its power and prestige. Its enormous wealth rested on its agricultural production, on international trade, and on the gold mined in its Nubian territories. Egypt was considered to be an inexhaustible source of gold at this time, and gold was freely used to ratify political treaties with foreign kings.

Amenhotep's reign was an era of great architectural works. Amenhotep built temples in Thebes and Nubia, and on the western bank of the Nile, near Luxor, he constructed both an enormous funerary temple and a new palace facing an artificial lake. Amenhotep's foreign policy relied mainly on negotiation, and his long reign was largely peaceful. Some of his diplomatic correspondence has been preserved on 400 clay tablets known as the Amarna Letters.

Amenhotep IV (ruled 1353–1335 BCE) is chiefly remembered for the major religious reformation that he introduced. To the consternation of the priests of Amon, Amenhotep decreed that the sun god Re (Re-Harakhte of Heliopolis) should be the sole god in

THE AMARNA LETTERS

When Akhenaton's capital city Akhetaton was abandoned around 1335 BCE, many things were left behind, including an archive of royal correspondence. This archive contained some 400 clay tablets inscribed in Babylonian, which was the predominant international language in western Asia in the 14th century BCE.

The tablets were found in 1887 CE by a peasant in the city of Tel el Amarna, which is on the site of the ancient Egyptian city of Akhetaton. The tablets have provided historians with important information about the Amarna period.

The tablets contain part of the correspondence between foreign rulers and the pharaohs Amenhotep III and his son and successor Amenhotep IV, who later became known as Akhenaton. The foreign rulers included the kings of Babylon, Assyria, and Mitanni, all of whom regarded the pharaoh as their equal and addressed him as "my brother." The rulers of city-states in the region of present-day Lebanon, Palestine, and Israel adopted a more deferential tone. These small princes were unpredictable factors in the power game, because they would ally themselves first with one major power and then with another.

The letters clearly show how the older states were being exposed to new threats. These threats included the great Hittite Empire, which was one of the earliest civilizations in Anatolia (roughly present-day Turkey) and was constantly seeking to extend its territories. Another threat was posed by the roaming Chabiru tribes, who may have been the Hebrews of the Bible. Some of the letters describe how a former vassal of Egypt, Abdi-Ashirta of Amurru, formed an alliance with the Chabiru and later with the Hittites. On the other hand, King Rib-Addi of Byblos remained loyal to the pharaoh and repeatedly wrote to the Egyptian king urging him to send troops quickly to prevent Abdi-Ashirta and other kings from joining forces against Egypt.

In addition to the political information they contain, the letters are valuable for the light they shed on the language of the time. The Canaanite writers did not use pure Babylonian; they used a mixture of Babylonian and their own language. The suffixes of the verbs used by these writers greatly resemble those of the much later Hebrew of the Bible, so the Amarna Letters provide a valuable link in tracing the development of this language.

This relief from a stele depicts the pharaoh Akhenaton and his wife and children. Above is the sun god Aton.

Egyptian religion. It was not unusual for one god to be considered preeminent, but Amenhotep's unprecedented decree denied the existence of any other divinities, bringing monotheism to Egypt. The temples of the old gods were abandoned, and their images were smashed.

Amenhotep also decreed that the god should be worshipped under a new name, Aton (or Aten), meaning "the disc of the sun." He changed his own name to Akhenaton (meaning "Servant of Aton")

and, as the son of Aton, announced that he was the only prophet of the new religion. This major religious change was marked by the celebration of the *sed* (or royal jubilee) in the fourth year after Akhenaton's accession, although the jubilee traditionally did not take place until the 30th year of a pharaoh's reign.

Aton was portrayed as the disk of the sun, a glowing circle devoid of all human features. This was a symbol taken from earlier depictions of Re. Images from

Akhenaton's time show the disk with long radiating rays that end in hands holding the ankh—the symbol of life. Akhenaton bestowed royal status on the god by writing his name in cartouches, the pictorial oval frames that were reserved for the names of royalty.

The pharaoh had a special temple built for Aton at Karnak, and to honor the god further, Akhenaton left Thebes and built a new capital city called Akhetaton (meaning "Aton's Horizon") near present-day Tel el Amarna in central Egypt. From the evidence of the stone monuments that mark the city limits, it dates from the sixth year of his reign. It served as the country's capital until Akhenaton's death. The royal court that took up residence in the new city consisted mainly of new people. Akhenaton may have wanted to distance himself from the former priests and officials.

The Amarna period lasted through the end of the 18th dynasty. However, the period was so reviled by Egyptian historians that the names of Akhenaton and his immediate successors were left out of the official royal lists. In one very rare case where Akhenaton is mentioned, he is called the "Enemy from Akhetaton."

Art and letters

There were many other changes during Akhenaton's reign in addition to the religious reformation. In art, many of the traditional conventions were abandoned, and things were portrayed more realistically, particularly the human figure. The surviving pictures of Akhenaton are very unflattering. They show a man with a narrow face, a potbelly, wide hips, and matchstick legs. In contrast, a bust of Akhenaton's wife Nefertiti depicts a woman of extraordinary beauty.

In literature, some forms of the spoken language were introduced, and the variation now known as Late Egyptian emerged as the standard written language

around 1380 BCE. It was used for business and some priestly documents until around 700 BCE. Classic Middle Egyptian continued to be used in religious texts.

The evidence of the Amarna Letters shows that Akhenaton maintained con-

This is a copy of a bust depicting Nefertiti, wife of Akhenaton.

tacts with other states through correspondence and the exchange of gifts, but it is clear that he failed to take decisive military action when Egypt began to lose its influence in the Syro-Palestinian region. There were also difficulties at home, caused by the closing of the temples, which effectively transferred the property of the temples to the pharaoh. Without the help of the local temple officials, it proved difficult to collect the income that arose from this property.

The mask of Tutankhamen from 1323 BCE is ancient Egypt's greatest treasure, but Tutankhamen was a relatively minor ruler.

Tutankhamen

Smenkhkare (ruled 1335–1332 BCE) reversed the religious reformation carried out by his predecessor and began building temples again in Thebes. He was succeeded after a brief reign by the nine-year-old Tutankhaten, who married Akhenaton's daughter Ankhesenaten and completed the break with the Aton cult by returning the capital to Memphis and by repairing and rebuilding the abandoned temples throughout the country. The pharaoh also marked the break with the past symbolically by changing his own name to Tutankhamen and that of his wife to Ankhesenamen.

Tutankhamen died young and was buried in a small, exquisitely decorated tomb in the Valley of the Kings. It seems that this tomb may have been forgotten, possibly due to the erasure of the Amarna period from the Egyptian memory. At any rate, it escaped the plundering suffered by all the other royal graves and was discovered virtually untouched in 1922 CE by the British archaeologists Howard Carter and Lord Carnarvon. Like the other royal tombs, its walls were covered with carved and painted hieroglyphics and representational scenes. Although it had apparently been robbed twice, it still held more than 5,000 items.

Power struggle

When he died at the age of 18 in 1323 BCE, Tutankhamen left a grieving widow, Ankhesenamen, and a throne that immediately became the stake in a power struggle. In the absence of a male heir, it seemed that the successor was bound to be a high-ranking official. Two possible candidates were Aya, an old official who had served Akhenaton, and a general, Horemheb. Rather than accepting either of them as her husband and the new pharaoh, Ankhesenamen wrote to the Hittite king Suppiluliumas, asking for one of his sons to ascend the Egyptian

throne. Suppiluliumas sent his son Zannanza, but the boy was assassinated before he reached Egypt, an act that may have been ordered by Aya, who promptly took the throne and sent Horemheb north to repel the incensed Hittites.

Aya lived for only another four years, and then Horemheb came to power in 1319 BCE. During his reign, he concentrated on domestic issues. He introduced reforms in the army and in the judicial system, and he reorganized the collection of taxes. Horemheb died around 1292 BCE, and his death marked the end of the 18th dynasty.

The Ramesside period

The first king of the 19th dynasty was Ramses I, who had been a general in Horemheb's army and had been appointed by him as his successor. After a short reign of two years, Ramses died and was succeeded by his son, Seti I (ruled 1290–1279 BCE).

Seti led successful military campaigns to restore Egypt's authority in Syria and Palestine and defeated tribes from the Libyan desert that were threatening Egypt's delta. A military engagement with the powerful Hittites ended in a treaty. At home, Seti began the construc-

Archaeologist Howard Carter (left) examines the innermost coffin of Tutankhamen in 1922 CE.

41

tion of a great hall for the temple of Amon at Karnak, and in the city of Abydos, he built a magnificent temple of white limestone (decorated with delicately painted reliefs), dedicated to himself and the god Osiris. He was succeeded by his son Ramses II.

Ramses II (ruled 1279–1213 BCE) continued his father's attempts to regain control of parts of Africa and western Asia that had been held by Egypt in previous centuries. The northern border, which continued to be threatened by the Hittites, was his main source of concern. The Hittites had occupied the city of Kadesh in Syria. In 1275 BCE, Ramses fought the Hittites at the Battle of Kadesh in an attempt to regain that territory. Scenes from the battle as portrayed on temple walls give the impression that the Egyptians were victorious, but the result was inconclusive. Ramses continued his campaign against the Hittites for the next 15 years, eventually concluding a treaty with them. The peace was ratified by a marriage between Ramses and a Hittite princess.

At home, Ramses proved to be an energetic builder of temples and monuments. He expanded the temple at Luxor and finished the great hall begun by his father in the temple of Amon at Karnak. He built a temple for himself at Abydos and an enormous mortuary temple at Thebes. New monuments were constructed in Nubia with colossal statues of himself. The best known of these is the rock-hewn temple of Abu Simbel. He also built a new capital in the eastern delta called Pi-Ramesse.

The Sea Peoples

Ramses was succeeded by his 13th son, Merneptah (ruled 1213–1204 BCE), who inherited an empire whose western approaches were being threatened by the Libyans. There was also a new threat from the north from the so-called Sea Peoples, who consisted of a number of groups that menaced the eastern Mediterranean coast. In the fifth year of Merneptah's reign, he fought off an invasion by the Libyans and Sea Peoples in the western delta, taking many captives who were later conscripted into the Egyptian army.

After Merneptah died in 1204 BCE, various members of the royal family competed to win the succession, resulting in a chaotic period that lasted until 1190 BCE—when Setnakht took the throne, founding the 20th dynasty.

Setnakht ruled for only a short time, from 1190 to 1187 BCE, and most of his reign was taken up with trying to restore order in a troubled kingdom. His son Ramses III (ruled 1187–1156 BCE) inherited a stable society and was the New Kingdom's last great pharaoh.

In this wall painting from the tomb of Tutankhamen, the pharaoh is welcomed into the land of the gods by the goddess Nut.

Although his kingdom was internally secure, Ramses III was harassed by continuing attempts at invasion by the Libyans and the Sea Peoples. Ramses successfully repulsed these invasions in a series of land and naval battles, but the military campaigns put a great strain on the Egyptian economy, and after Ramses' death, the kingdom began to decline.

The priests and the army

The reigns of the later Ramesside kings saw a major increase in the power of two groups—the priests and the army. The temples were major owners of land, and the priests profited from this, becoming virtually independent from the central bureaucracy. In particular, the temple of Amon at Karnak became so powerful that it practically controlled Upper Egypt. Because the office of priest was hereditary, the high priests became a dynasty to rival the royal dynasty.

To defend Egypt's borders, the pharaohs had built up a powerful standing army. This army was augmented by mercenaries, who were often prisoners of war who had agreed to fight for Egypt. These mercenaries were established in military colonies, and in time, they became a significant political force in the kingdom.

The increasing power of the army and the priests of Amon put an end to the New Kingdom around 1075 BCE. During a time of civil unrest in Thebes, the pharaoh sent Panehsi, the viceroy of Kush, to restore order. However, he was unsuccessful; Herihor, a new high priest of Amon, took control of the Theban region and claimed to be king, while the pharaoh looked on helplessly from his distant residence in the Nile Delta.

The Third Intermediate period

The Third Intermediate period (c. 1075–664 BCE) ran from the 21st dynasty to the 25th dynasty. The beginning of the 21st dynasty saw the country divided. The first king, Smendes, ruled from Tanis in the northeastern delta, while the Theban priests controlled the south. The pharaoh was represented in Thebes by one of his daughters, who assumed the title "Divine Wife of Amon." Thebes eventually became a separate state (the "Divine State of Amon") guided by the high priests and the wives of the god. As such, it continued to exist even after the

This colossal statue from the 13th century BCE depicts Ramses II, one of the greatest of the New Kingdom pharaohs.

WOMEN IN ANCIENT EGYPT

Women enjoyed a far higher status in ancient Egypt than in most other early societies. In many aspects, they were considered the equal of men; they had the right to own land, represent themselves in legal proceedings, and conduct a business.

Young girls remained at home with their mothers to receive training in domestic duties and household management. Unlike boys, girls were never sent to school, but they might be taught to read and write at home. Girls from peasant families were usually married when they were around 12 years old; girls from better-off families married a little later. Marriages were generally arranged, although the young people might have some say in the matter. Before a marriage took place in richer families, the couple signed a pre-nuptial agreement, which stipulated that the husband was to pay an allowance to his wife and that any material possessions she brought to the marriage would remain hers if the marriage ended.

For girls who did not marry, other opportunities were available. Some single women became singers, musicians, dancers, or acrobats. Others might find employment with a wealthy family as a maid or nanny, while a girl from a noble family could become a priestess.

For most women, daily work consisted of looking after the home and children. Wheat had to be ground into flour, which was then made into bread and baked in a clay oven. Other food, such as fish, meat, and vegetables, might be boiled or roasted over an open fire. A mother would generally weave flax into linen and then make clothes for her family—men generally wore a short skirt called a kilt and women wore a straight dress held up with straps.

Egyptians placed great emphasis on cleanliness, and both women and men would bathe daily, either in the river or in a basin of water in the house. They then anointed themselves with perfumed oil and applied face makeup.

The temple complex at Abu Simbel, carved out of the mountainside during the reign of Ramses II (ruled 1279–1213 BCE), is one of Egypt's most popular tourist attractions.

other parts of Egypt were defeated by other nations.

During the 21st dynasty, Libyan principalities arose in the Nile Delta, and in 950 BCE, a Libyan military leader named Sheshonk seized the throne, establishing the 22nd dynasty (950–730 BCE). While the Libyans consolidated their position in the north by establishing military garrisons, they attempted to improve relations with Thebes through political marriages with priestly families. Thebes continued to resent the northern dynasty, however, and eventually established the rival 23rd dynasty in the south.

The latter part of the 22nd dynasty was characterized by an increasing fragmentation of land and by power struggles. In 730 BCE, a Kushite ruler called Piye raided as far north as Memphis, and the northern rulers were forced to pay him tribute. However, after Piye returned to Kush, the Libyan prince Tefnakhte of Sais reassertd his claims in the north. His son Bocchoris succeeded him as the sole pharaoh of the 24th dynasty (c. 722–715 BCE). The Libyan domination was finally ended by Piye's brother Shabaka, who succeeded in bringing the whole of Egypt under his control and founded the 25th dynasty.

The Late period

Egypt remained under Nubian rule for almost 50 years, and it was a time of internal peace and prosperity. However, the might of Assyria had been growing since the ninth century, and in 671 BCE, the Assyrian king Esarhaddon invaded Egypt and took Memphis. For the next several years, campaigns were fought on Egyptian soil between Assyrians and Egyptian kings, but problems at home eventually forced the Assyrians to withdraw, leaving Psamtik I to inaugurate the 26th dynasty (664–525 BCE). Under Psamtik, north and south were united once more.

In 525 BCE, the Persians conquered Egypt, and the Persian king Cambyses became the first ruler of the 27th dynasty. The country remained under Persian domination until 404 BCE. Native Egyptian rulers then reasserted their independence through the next three dynasties. The 31st dynasty saw a return to Persian rule, which held until Alexander the Great conquered Egypt in 332 BCE, making it part of the Greek world.

This hallway leads to the tomb of Ramses VI, who reigned in the 12th century BCE.

See also:

The Assyrians (page 102) • Egypt's Middle Kingdom (page 14) • Egypt's Old Kingdom (page 6) • The Hittites (page 78) • The Persians (page 126)

THE SUMERIANS

S umer was one of the world's first major civilizations. For most of its history, it was made up of a number of independent city-states. However, under the Akkadian king Sargon the Great, it was a unified, powerful, and prosperous empire.

The area of western Asia that is today covered by the country of Iraq gave birth to several ancient civilizations, including Sumer, Akkad, and Babylon. All of these cultures grew up in the south of the modern country in an area bounded by two great rivers, the Euphrates and the Tigris. The Greeks named this region Mesopotamia, meaning "the land between two rivers."

Early farmers

Archaeological evidence (see box, page 59) has revealed that a Semitic-speaking people, probably from the deserts of Arabia and Syria, began to populate the southern part of Mesopotamia around 5000 BCE. These people were attracted by the low-lying plains of fertile soil between the two rivers. However, although the rivers flooded the valley every spring, there was virtually no rainfall during the summer, making it impossible to grow crops successfully. Nevertheless, the incomers were resourceful people, and they soon learned how to build reservoirs to store the flood water and canals to carry it to the fields. With an effective system of irrigation in place, they were able to grow crops such as wheat, barley, and dates, and their communities thrived.

Society gradually became more complex as the villages found it necessary to cooperate with each other to maintain their network of irrigation canals. The settlements became larger as the population increased, and with the threat of attack from foreign tribes, it soon became expedient to build fortified walls. Around 4500 BCE, the first cities emerged, the largest of which, Uruk (see box, page 57), gave its name to this pre-Sumerian era.

The Sumerians

From around 3400 BCE, a distinctive Sumerian culture began to emerge. The difference between the Sumerians and their predecessors was purely linguistic. The Sumerians used a unique language of their own that became the common speech of their society, one of the foremost early civilizations. The Sumerian culture was strong and vibrant, with a highly organized social structure and a set of complex belief systems. Above all, the Sumerians were pioneers of writing and mathematics.

From the middle of the fourth millennium BCE onward, the cities of Sumer began to grow in size and number. Besides Uruk, they included Ur,

This harp, found in the royal tombs at Ur, has been partially restored. Although its main body is modern, the gold decorative head of a bull is around 4,500 years old.

46

THE SUMERIAN WORLD

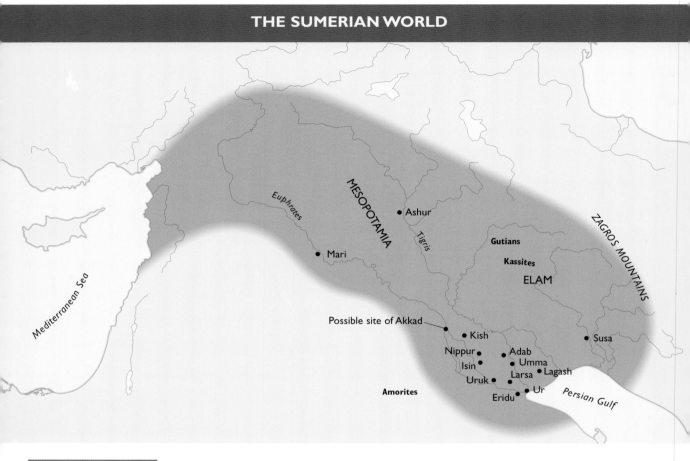

KEY

Area of Sumerian cultural influence

Nippur, Adab, Eridu, Isin, Kish, Lagash, and Larsa. There was no central government to unite these cities. Each city was independent, although their inhabitants all thought of themselves as being Sumerian. The temple in each city occupied a crucial position in Sumerian life. The god of the temple was considered to be the giver of fertility, and the temple itself owned most of the city's lands and herds of cattle.

Reflecting its important sociological position, the temple was the most conspicuous structure in any town or village. It usually consisted of a number of terraces, forming the typical Mesopotamian temple tower called a ziggurat. During the Uruk period, temples were decorated with mosaics. These mosaics consisted of cones made of clay or stone with colored tips that were hammered into the clay walls to create colorful patterns.

Social structure

The highest authority in a city was originally the *ensi*, a kind of governor who reigned on behalf of the temple god. Gradually, as the areas that belonged to a city grew, the cities became city-states, rather like the later city-states of ancient Greece. A new political figure emerged—the *lugal* (usually translated as "great man" or simply "king"). It is possible that a *lugal* was originally appointed during a time of war, and the position then became permanent.

Helping the *lugal* to retain his power was a body of personal soldier slaves, who belonged to the *lugal* outright. Most of these slaves had been captured in battle and owed their lives to the king. The king kept them close to him at all times, even eating with them in his palace, and they served him faithfully, both by fighting for him in times of war and by working on the building of public projects in peacetime.

The Early Dynastic period

The earliest period of Sumerian history that is reliably recorded is the Early Dynastic period (c. 2750–2335 BCE). At this time, Sumer was divided into several city-states that were often at war with one another, usually because of disputes over water rights and land.

The earliest *lugal* for whom a historical record has been discovered is Enmebaragesi, king of Kish, who ruled from around 2630 to 2600 BCE. Kish was one of the more important Sumerian city-states, and an ancient Sumerian poem entitled *Gilgamesh and Agga of Kish* relates how Enmebaragesi's son, Agga, besieged the city of Uruk. However, it appears he was not successful, because in the Sumerian king list, he is shown to be the last king of his dynasty. The ruler of Uruk subsequently became the overlord of Kish.

Despite the constant battles between the city-states, a great flowering of the arts and architecture occurred in this period. One of the most spectacular archaeological discoveries from Early Dynastic Sumer was the royal cemetery at Ur, which was uncovered by the archaeologist Sir Leonard Woolley during his excavations of the city in the 1920s CE. This cemetery contained hundreds of burials, dating from between 2600 and 2400 BCE. The graves contained the personal possessions of the deceased, and 17 of them were much more elaborate than the others; Woolley called these the royal tombs. The graves contained a wealth of precious objects fashioned in silver and gold, together

The town of Mosul stands on the banks of the Tigris River. Many of the great cities of ancient Mesopotamia lay on the banks of either the Tigris or the Euphrates.

The Ziggurat of Ur, once the focal point of the city's religious practices, has been fully restored.

with furniture, musical instruments, carts, draft animals, and even the bodies of servants who had been sacrificed to accompany the tomb owner into the afterlife. In one remarkable tomb, 74 royal attendants were found, all magnificently dressed and adorned.

One of the most fascinating of all the finds was a small wooden box inlaid with shell and lapis lazuli. This box, now known as the Standard of Ur, bears on its sides inlaid pictures of Sumerian life. One long side shows a scene of a royal feast, while the other depicts a battle scene. The box's end panels are also inlaid; one shows scenes of the sacrifice of a ram to the gods.

A time of war

Throughout the Early Dynastic period, there was constant warfare between the city-states. In particular, there was a long-running dispute over a boundary between Lagash and Umma. Eannatum of Lagash achieved an important victory in 2425 BCE. However, during the reign of his successor, Umma once again invaded Lagash territory, only to be defeated and driven back by the Lagash crown prince, Entemena. The friction continued for generations.

In 2351 BCE, Uruinimgina came to the throne of Lagash. He was a remarkable social reformer who, according to the cuneiform records, reinstated many temple privileges. He had a new attitude toward his fellow men, forgiving the debts of small farmers and reducing the power of the bureaucrats. However, his reign was marred by a catastrophic raid by Lugalzaggisi, the ruler of Umma, who eventually succeeded in destroying the kingdom of Lagash. For a time, Lugalzaggisi reigned as the strongest ruler in southern Mesopotamia, well on the way to achieving full control over the whole of Sumer. However, his plans were foiled by a young king from the north called Sargon.

A legendary infancy

Historians know little about Sargon's background. One legend relates that he was abandoned as an infant by his mother, a high priestess in the service of the Akkadian goddess Ishtar. The child was placed in a basket and set adrift on the Euphrates River, where he was found by a fruit grower named Aggi who brought him up. The legend goes on to say that, in his youth, Sargon became a cupbearer in the court of the king of Kish. Then, with the help of Ishtar, Sargon managed to free himself from the king and found a new dynasty.

War between Lugalzaggisi and Sargon was inevitable. Texts discovered by archaeologists list many battles between the two kings. Sargon triumphed eventually and conquered the rest of southern Mesopotamia as well, tearing down the walls of the cities he defeated. Sargon then marched to the edge of the Persian Gulf and washed his weapons in the water to show that he was the master of all the land between Kish and the coast.

Sargon built a new capital city on the banks of the Euphrates River. He called the city Akkad (or Agade), and although the remains of the city have never been found, it is believed to have been near the present-day city of Baghdad. The Akkadian Empire was established around 2335 BCE, and by the end of his reign in 2279 BCE, Sargon (or Sargon the Great as he was later called) had made Akkad the greatest city in Mesopotamia. His Akkadians and the people of northern Sumer gradually merged to produce a new, highly advanced civilization that left a considerable and lasting mark on Mesopotamian culture.

Sargon's empire

Sargon's newly erected capital had none of the prestige of Sumer's ancient cities. Nevertheless, thanks to its position on the Euphrates, Akkad soon became a thriving trading center. People flocked to it from all over the empire, bringing goods such as grain and livestock to trade. At the same time, ships from faraway India and Egypt brought exotic goods to sell. Sargon was quick to exploit the city's pivotal position. Because he

Made around 2600 BCE, the Standard of Ur is one of the most famous treasures of ancient Mesopotamia. Archaeologists are still unsure of its purpose; some have suggested it was the sounding box of a musical instrument.

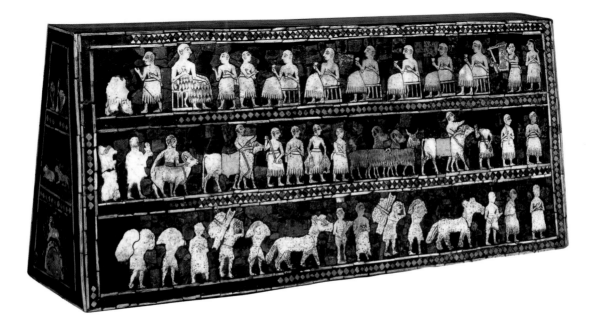

needed to procure most of his raw materials from outside Mesopotamia, he established a state monopoly over the supply routes. To this end, he took control of the upper Euphrates River, conquering a number of cities in the process, including Mari. Sargon also made the trade in tin, which was essential for the manufacture of bronze, a state monopoly.

Sargon led other campaigns, including one to Elam in the east—forcing the Elamites to move their capital to Susa. In the west, he campaigned in Syria and Lebanon, which gained him access to valuable resources such as cedar wood and silver.

Akkadian culture

Sargon initiated one of the most splendid eras of Mesopotamian culture. The Akkadians assimilated the Sumerian culture without giving up their own identity. One particularly important aspect was that the Semitic language now developed a written form—known today as Akkadian cuneiform—which was similar to Sumerian writing (see box, page 60).

Although Akkad, the city that gave the era its name, has never been discovered, there have been many archaeological finds from the Akkadian period. These finds include a great many cylinder seals of exceptional quality and a smaller number of stele (inscribed stone pillars). The images depicted on these artifacts show significant differences between Sumerian and Akkadian artists. Whereas Sumerian artists were mainly concerned with depicting religious scenes, the Akkadians tended to portray more historical events. The victory stele of King Naram-Sin, for

This elaborate gold and lapis lazuli headdress was once worn by Queen Puabi, who lived in the city of Ur in the late third millennium BCE.

example, shows the king storming the mountains and the defeated Lullubi falling down them.

One ruler

The main political difference between the Akkadian Empire and the preceding Sumerian period was the establishment of a unified government. Although the Sumerian kings had been moving in that direction for centuries, none had ever achieved the dominance of Sargon. Instead of several more or less equal sovereigns vying for power, there was now a single ruler and a government structured like a pyramid, with the omnipotent king at the top. To keep a tight hold on his empire, Sargon gave most of the important positions to relatives and friends. The title *ensi* was now used to mean "deputy of the king" rather than "representative of the god."

Sargon also handed out land under loan agreements, with himself as the only landlord. This was completely different from the customs of the Sumerian city-states, where the gods, through the temples, were the major landowners. However, Sargon took great pains to justify his political and religious innovations on a theological level. He made his daughter Enheduanna the priestess of Nanna, the moon god, and with her help, the Akkadian goddess Ishtar was elevated from being the goddess of war to being the goddess of love and fertility. As such, she was identified with the Sumerian goddess Inanna.

King of the four quarters

The old Sumerian cities did not accept all of Sargon's innovations without resistance. When Sargon's youthful grandson Naram-Sin ascended the throne around 2254 BCE, the cities staged a rebellion. Naram-Sin managed to subdue it and then established garrisons in the far corners of his empire. Having achieved control over the whole of Mesopotamia, he extended his power to the surrounding regions and called himself "the king of the four quarters"—a title that would be assumed by later Mesopotamian kings to indicate their claim to a world empire.

Naram-Sin also claimed to be divine. He had himself portrayed wearing horned headgear (a sign of divinity), and when his name was written, it was preceded by a pictogram that indicated that the following combination of characters formed the name of a god. Naram-Sin even called himself the husband of the

This golden model of a ram climbing through a thicket, made around 2600 BCE, is a supreme example of Sumerian metalwork.

goddess Ishtar. Although such practices were common in contemporary societies such as Egypt, it was not customary to deify a king in Mesopotamia, and it was not to last. By the reign of the Babylonian ruler Hammurabi in the 18th century BCE, the king was once again presented as the first and most important servant of a deity rather than as a deity himself.

Under King Sharkalisharri (ruled c. 2217–2193 BCE), the Akkadian Empire went into decline. Sharkalisharri was attacked on all sides. In the northwest, he campaigned against the Amorites, while in the south, Uruk almost succeeded in gaining its independence. After the king's death, there were quarrels over who should succeed him, and the empire disintegrated.

The Gutians

During the last years of the Akkadian Empire, there were many incursions by fierce tribesmen from the southeast carrying out "hit-and-run" raids. These intruders were the Gutians, one of many peoples living in the Zagros Mountains. These raiders plundered the rich cities of the Mesopotamian plain and were always long gone before an army could arrive to confront them. The Gutians pillaged all over the Akkadian Empire, although they occupied only a few remote regions. Finally, they destroyed Akkad itself. A lamentation, supposedly

This bronze head depicts an Akkadian king, probably either Sargon or Naram-Sin.

spoken by the goddess Ishtar, attributes the destruction of the city to the vengeful god Enlil of Nippur, who was said to have called on the Gutians to punish Sargon's dynasty for its pride and impiety.

Gudea's reign

After the destruction of Akkad, Gutian kings took control of the Akkadian Empire but proved to be poor administrators. By the end of the Akkadian era, the southern part of Sumer, and the city of Uruk in particular, enjoyed a considerable measure of independence.

In the 22nd century BCE, the city-state of Lagash also became more important. Under the rule of Gudea (c. 2141–2122 BCE), a Sumerian renaissance began. Gudea undertook an extensive program of temple building, and splendid statues and royal monuments bearing his likeness have been recovered. He was known as a good administrator, ruling in accordance with the old Sumerian traditions. The fact that he assumed the title of *ensi* of Lagash—governor in the name of the god of Lagash—is indicative of his piety.

Gudea considered himself to be the servant of a god, not, like the Akkadian Naram-Sin, a deity in human form. The evidence for this comes in the form of a hymn describing the construction of the temple Eninnu at Girsu, the city of royal residence (see box, page 56).

Despite the grandeur of his reign, it was not Gudea but Utuhegal (ruled 2116–2112 BCE), king of Uruk, who succeeded in winning full independence from the Gutians. He inflicted a crushing defeat on the Gutians, not only annihilating the Gutian army but also destroying the boats in which the tribesmen had made their surprise raids. Freed from the Gutian scourge, southern Mesopotamia soon recovered from the economic paralysis caused by the invaders, and a feeling of Sumerian national pride emerged again. It was at this time that the Sumerian king list was composed. It cataloged the kings and rulers of cities from earliest times.

The Ur III period

The final flowering of the Sumerian civilization is usually called the Ur III period, after one of its major dynasties—the third dynasty of Ur, which was founded by Ur-Nammu, who was military governor of Ur under Utuhegal. After Utuhegal's death, Ur-Nammu became king, and the dynasty lasted for almost a hundred years.

Reigning from 2112 to 2095 BCE, Ur-Nammu first consolidated his position by taking over Lagash and its surrounding area. This move gave him control of a large part of southern Mesopotamia. Most of the remainder of his reign was peaceful, and he is remembered chiefly for instituting a major rebuilding program for the decaying temples, putting in place provincial governors to administer central government, and introducing an enlightened legal code some three centuries before the more famous one written by Hammurabi of Babylon.

Shulgi, Ur-Nammu's son, ruled from around 2094 to 2047 BCE and was noted for his skills as a soldier and a diplomat. He encouraged the building of

The victory stele of Naram-Sin portrays the king ascending a mountain to attack his enemies.

GUDEA'S BUILDING HYMN

Gudea's building hymn on the construction of the Eninnu temple, dedicated to the god Ningirsu, is the longest known Sumerian text. Written on two clay cylinders, each 12 inches (30 cm) high, the hymn runs to more than 1,360 lines and describes a year of continuous drought, during which the crops wither and the mountain streams disappear. Gudea realizes that famine is imminent, and as the emergency reaches its peak, he has a dream in which the god Ningirsu appears. After Gudea has reverently addressed him as "my king," Ningirsu tells him: "In my city (Girsu) water does not run through the canals; the water does not shine; the canal does not have water like the Tigris. Therefore, build a temple, the most beautiful on earth and in heaven."

Gudea agrees to do this, but in order to understand the dream better, he visits a temple and offers sacrifices. While he is deep in prayer before her statue, the goddess Nanshe appears and explains the dream more fully. She says that Gudea needs to make more offerings and that the god Ningirsu will then provide him with more details about the temple.

Gudea then places valuable objects at the foot of the statue and lies down before it to await instructions. Ningirsu approaches him, and when Gudea gets to his feet, they converse as friends. The god gives Gudea explicit information about the

dimensions of the rooms in the temple and the way it should be constructed. He promises that when the temple is completed, water will again run through the canals and the land will be fertile.

Gudea follows the god's advice to the letter, and his laborers work day and night to construct the temple. The king dispatches major expeditions to the mountains for pine and cedar and sends others in search of building stone. He also has copper, gold, silver, marble, and porphyry brought in from the surrounding lands.

The building hymn goes on to describe how Gudea himself molds the first clay tile for the temple and holds it high up to let it dry in the sun. He places a carrying basket on his head "as if it were a holy crown."

The hymn ends with an extensive description of the inauguration ceremonies of the new temple. These involve many offerings and day-long festivities. The hymn describes how Ningirsu finally takes possession of the temple "like a hurricane," accompanied by a parade of lesser gods, including one leading a triumphal chariot, a shepherd, a musician, the inspector of fisheries, and Ningirsu's architect and steward. All these gods are servants to Ningirsu, for whom Gudea has built the Eninnu. The extensive retinue probably offers a valid picture of Gudea's own throng of servants and courtiers.

This statue depicts Gudea, who ruled Lagash in the 22nd century BCE. Gudea built a famous temple to the god Ningirsu.

new schools and was a patron of literature. During his long reign, education flourished. Shulgi's reign was for the most part peaceful, allowing him the opportunity to improve communications within his realm by maintaining the road system and establishing rest houses at regular intervals for travelers. Toward the end of his reign, however, raids from aggressive tribes in the west prompted Shulgi to build a fortified wall to protect his northwest borders.

The last king of the dynasty was Ibbi-Sin, who reigned from 2028 to 2004

The Warka Vase, made in Uruk sometime between 3200 and 3000 BCE, is one of Mesopotamia's oldest treasures.

THE CITY OF URUK

The city of Uruk, which gave its name to the pre-Sumerian period, dates from around 4500 BCE, when it probably held around 1,000 people. Over the next 1,500 years, it grew into an enormous city covering 250 acres (100 ha). It was surrounded by 6 miles (9 km) of mud-brick walls, built to protect the inhabitants from raids by nomadic tribesmen. All the dwellings in the city were constructed of mud bricks dried in the sun. The more important citizens such as the priests and noblemen probably had fairly grand houses, but the ordinary citizens lived in simple one- or two-room constructions. The main buildings in the city were the temples, dedicated to Anu, the sky god, and Inanna, goddess of love and war. These temples were built on a massive earth terrace that occupied one-third of the area of the city.

Some historians think that the temples began life as warehouses for storing the harvest from the surrounding areas. The community's sacred objects would also have been kept there, so that they gradually became the locations of religious ceremonies. Because the priests were the intermediaries between the citizens and the gods, they soon began to control the running of the city, receiving crops from the farmers, some of which they sacrificed to the gods and some of which they traded for other goods.

The inhabitants of Uruk were resourceful and inventive people. The Uruk metalsmiths learned how to extract copper from copper ore. Later, they found out how to make a harder metal, bronze, by heating copper and tin together. Uruk farmers greatly improved their farming methods by using a plow with metal, rather than wooden, blades and by getting a team of oxen, rather than men, to pull it. Uruk potters invented the potter's wheel—a wooden turntable that rotated, making it much easier to fashion clay pots. Later, the wheel was put to use on a cart that could be pulled by a donkey or mule, introducing arguably the world's first method of wheeled transportation.

BCE. At first, his reign was uneventful. Then, a disastrous incursion by the tribes that the wall was meant to keep out resulted in chaos and a breakdown in internal administration. One catastrophe followed another. While Ibbi-Sin was waging war against the Elamites in the southeast, one of his generals, Ishbi-Irra, rebelled and started to appropriate parts of Ur's realm. In 2004 BCE, the Elamites invaded southern Mesopotamia and laid siege to Ur itself. Weakened by hunger, the defenders capitulated and were all ruthlessly massacred. The city was sacked, and Ibbi-Sin was taken captive. The event effectively marked the end of the Sumerian civilization.

Sumerian religion

Sumerian religion was pantheistic in nature, meaning that it involved the worship of a great number of gods. All of them looked like humans but had superhuman characteristics. The gods were considered to be human in certain respects: they lived in a house (the temple), ate food (provided by sacrifices), married human women (the temple priestesses), and had children by them. However, the gods were also immortal and had magical powers over the lives of their worshipers. In particular, they could deliver success in battle and at harvest time.

The Sumerians believed in four major gods of creation, each responsible for a different aspect of the universe. Anu, god of the heavens, had his main temple in Uruk. Ki was the goddess of earth, while Enlil, the god of air, wind, and rain, controlled prosperity and adversity and personified the floods that

The man depicted in this ancient votive (praying) figure is wearing clothes of goat skin.

could bring both fertility and destruction. Enlil's temple, the most important in Sumer, was found at Nippur. Enki was the god of the deep waters and also the god of wisdom who brought knowledge of crafts and writing. His temple was the Apsu at Eridu, and he was said to have created the earth and the people from the clay of the Apsu.

Below these four principle gods were three lesser deities. Nanna, the moon god, was father of the other two—Utu, the sun god, and Inanna, the goddess of heaven, love, procreation, and war. Every city had one of these gods as its patron, and a temple was dedicated to that god. Temple ceremonies, including sacrifices, were held daily. There were also innumerable other deities, including gods associated with specific mountains, plains, and rivers. There were even gods for individual tools like plows and axes.

Inanna and Dumu-zi

The Sumerian myth to explain the seasons involved the marriage of the mortal male Dumu-zi to the goddess Inanna. The marriage was intended to protect the fertility of both the land and the people. Dumu-zi, however, failed to please his wife. Dissatisfied and angry, she ordered him to be banished to the underworld for half of every year, which created a dry season when nothing could grow. Dumu-zi returned to his wife at the fall equinox, when day and night were of equal length and the seasons changed. His return allowed all life on earth to be renewed and the land to become fertile again. This was the time of the new year

ARCHAEOLOGY

The existence of the Sumerian civilization was not even suspected until the middle of the 19th century CE. It was then that archaeologists excavating the Assyrian sites of Nineveh, Dur Sharrukin, and Calah discovered thousands of clay tablets dating from the first millennium BCE and inscribed in Akkadian cuneiform. Others were in an unknown language. The French archaeologist Jules Oppert named the unknown language Sumerian because of the frequent mention of the king of Sumer. Further knowledge of Sumerian history was gleaned from clay tablets and artifacts found at other Sumerian cities.

There remains a perennial problem with dating these finds accurately. Because the inhabitants of southern Mesopotamia did not have natural stone for building, they had to rely on bricks made of clay. These clay bricks would eventually fuse with a building's foundations, leaving only a single compact mass of clay. A very refined technique is thus required to identify the original layers. The ancient practice of constructing new buildings directly on top of the remains of the old ones further complicates matters.

The same practice of building new on top of old was used for entire cities, so building levels became increasingly higher, forming hills known as tells. Although many of these tells have been explored, no one has yet been able to reach the remains of the earliest human settlements in the region because the groundwater level has risen. The deepest layers reached to date reveal evidence of a people who had complex belief systems and social organization and who used a primitive pictographic system of writing. These earliest inhabitants arrived around 5000 BCE and were the ancestors of the Sumerians.

Archaeologist Leonard Woolley carries an ancient harp discovered in the royal tombs at Ur in 1929 CE.

THE DEVELOPMENT OF WRITING

The Sumerian system of writing appears to have evolved out of a number of different recording systems developed in southern Mesopotamia. The original impetus for developing writing was the need to keep accounts. At first a simple picture script, the system allowed the number of sheep, goats, or baskets of grain brought to the temple to be recorded.

The style of script used by the Sumerians is called cuneiform (wedge-shaped) because it was written by pressing a pointed stick, or stylus, into a tablet of soft clay, leaving an impression in the shape of a wedge. The tablets were then dried in the sun or fired, and they could last for thousands of years.

To begin with, the cuneiform style of writing was pictographic, which meant that each sign of the script represented an object or, later, an idea. Eventually, these pictorial signs changed into phonetic symbols. So, for example, in the first phase, the symbol for a star was also the symbol for a god. The same sign was used for "An," which means either heaven or the god Anu. In the next phase, the star symbol came to represent the syllable "an," even in words that had nothing to do with the god, a star, or heaven.

The development of writing was crucial to the development of civilizations. It permitted the keeping of permanent records and the transmission of information over large distances—both essential to a civilization ruled by a central

administration. The cuneiform script was universally adopted by the early Mesopotamian civilizations and remained the basic form of written communication in western Asia for the next 2,000 years.

The cuneiform writing on this Sumerian tablet, from the time of the third dynasty of Ur, lists plowmen employed by the state and the amount of land that was assigned to them as wages.

in Sumerian culture, and it was celebrated by a reenactment of the wedding of Dumu-zi and Inanna. The myth has parallels to the Greek story of Persephone, Hades, and Demeter, which also explains the origins of the seasons.

Education

The Sumerians needed to train a large body of scribes to carry out the administration of the empire, and for this purpose, schools were attached to most of the temples. Both boys and girls were taught how to write the cuneiform script, something that was not easily mastered. The script had hundreds of signs, many of which had more than one meaning. The students' tablets that have been recovered indicate something of the immensity of the task. The student had to memorize long lists of signs together with their phonetic values, plus lists of ideograms, which represented a single word or idea. After that, the student had to learn grammar and practice writing short sentences.

This dagger and gold sheath were found in the royal tombs at Ur.

Apart from learning to write the cuneiform script, students were taught mathematics. The counting system used by the Sumerians was the duodecimal system, which probably predated the Sumerian period. This system uses 12 (which is divisible by six, four, three, and two) as its basic unit rather than 10 (as in the metric system). Aspects of the Mesopotamian system survive to this day, however; for example, a circle is divided into 360 degrees, the year has 12 months, and there are 60 minutes in an hour and 60 seconds in a minute. The Sumerian students learned multiplication and division tables and were familiar with tables that gave square and cube roots. They were taught about weights and measures and how to calculate the area of an irregular plot of ground.

Other students studied to enter a specialized profession such as that of an architect. After graduation, some students would be employed by the temple, while others would go into the civil service or be employed by private individuals.

See also:

The Babylonians (page 62)

THE BABYLONIANS

In the first and second millenniums BCE, the power and influence of the Mesopotamian city of Babylon fluctuated greatly. The periods of its greatest power came during the reigns of Hammurabi and Nebuchadnezzar II—more than a thousand years apart.

The fall of the third dynasty of Ur in 2004 BCE marked the start of a new period in Mesopotamian history—the Old Babylonian period, which lasted until the end of the first dynasty of Babylon in 1595 BCE. During this period, the Sumerian civilization declined, and Babylon became the political and cultural center of Mesopotamia.

In the first part of this period, semi-nomadic Amorite tribes from the western desert invaded the Mesopotamian plain and captured several cities. The ensuing battles between the invaders and the original inhabitants made this a time of great confusion. Eventually, two city-states came to prominence—Isin and Larsa. The victorious chiefs ruling the conquered cities established their own dynasties and, for the most part, assimilated the existing Sumerian culture.

The first dynasty of Babylon

Around 1894 BCE, an Amorite called Sumu-abu seized power in the Akkadian city of Babylon, founding the first dynasty of Babylon. At that time, Babylon was no more than a minor city in a highly unstable area, but over the next 100 years, the Babylonian kings consolidated their position, and when the sixth king of the dynasty, Hammurabi, came to the throne around 1792 BCE, he inherited a secure state with growing influence.

Hammurabi was an energetic young man with an outstanding gift for diplomacy and military strategy. During the 42 years of his reign, he transformed Babylon into the preeminent city of Mesopotamia and created an empire that extended from Assyria in the north to the Persian Gulf in the south. Arts and sciences flourished, making it the "golden age" of the Old Empire.

Initially, Hammurabi devoted himself to building temples and canals and establishing his code of law. For several years, he then concentrated on building cordial relations with neighboring rulers. In the 29th year of his reign, he switched tactics, changing to an aggressive policy of extending his empire by military means. In 1762 BCE, he conquered Larsa. He followed this by defeating the kings of Elam, Mari, and Eshnunna and two powerful kings in northern Mesopotamia, Shamshi-Adad I and Ishme-Dagan. He then annexed the whole of Sumer. In the north, he took control of Ashur and Nineveh, claiming the title "King of Sumer and Akkad."

Hammurabi's influence on the history of Mesopotamia was immense. Besides building a vast empire, he also made Babylon such an important Mesopotamian center that it remained the leading city of western Asia long after his death in 1750 BCE.

The Code of Hammurabi

According to the sources that have survived, Hammurabi was a fair and just ruler. From a central government in the city of Babylon, he cared for his subjects and defended the weak, even the inhabitants of two cities he destroyed—Mari and Eshnunna. He treated the people who lived there leniently and built new homes for those who had lost their dwellings. He took a personal interest in the affairs of the empire, supervising such matters as irrigation and agriculture, tax collection, and the construction of many buildings, especially temples.

One of Hammurabi's concerns was to ensure that the rule of law and justice was observed throughout his lands. To this end, he devised a collection of laws and edicts, which is now known as the Code of Hammurabi.

Although Ur-Nammu, king of Ur, had introduced what appears to be the first code of law in Mesopotamia some three centuries earlier, Hammurabi's code is the earliest known complete legal classification. Hammurabi claimed that his code was divinely inspired, but it

This relief of a bull, created in the sixth century BCE, once adorned the walls of Babylon. The Babylonians believed that bulls were sacred animals.

THE EMPIRE OF HAMMURABI

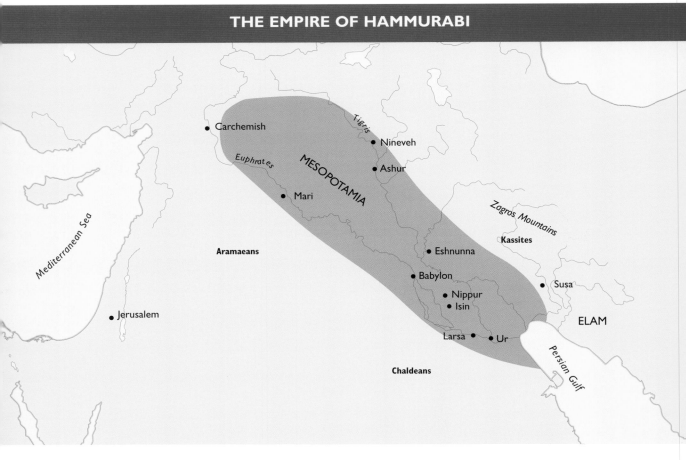

has now been established that it was rooted in an ancient Mesopotamian legal tradition that dated back to the time of the Sumerians.

The code was discovered in the winter of 1901–1902 CE by a French archaeological expedition that was excavating the ruins of Susa in southwest Iran (ancient Elam). The team unearthed three pieces of stone, which had obviously once made up a single block, engraved in cuneiform script. When restored, the stone blocks formed a stele carved out of black diorite and standing 7 feet 4 inches (2.2 m) high. It appears that the stele was stolen from Babylon by a king of Elam in 1158 BCE.

At the top of the stele is a relief that shows the sun god Shamash (who was associated with justice) handing Hammurabi a staff and ring, the emblems of his power to administer the law. Below the relief are 16 horizontal columns of cuneiform text in Akkadian, the Semitic language spoken in Mesopotamia at that time. On the reverse side, there are 28 further columns of text. The code consists of a prologue, a middle section containing the laws, and an epilogue.

Prologue and procedures

Hammurabi's code opens with a prologue, in which Hammurabi suggests that the gods have given him a special role as lawgiver and protector of the weak: "Anum and Enlil appointed me to promote the well-being of the people, me, Hammurabi, the pious, god-fearing ruler! To insure that law would rule in the whole land, to destroy the wicked and the evil so that the strong do not oppress the weak, to rise as the sun above the people and to light the land, Hammurabi, the people's shepherd, the one named by Enlil, that am I."

The prologue is followed by the laws themselves, divided into 28 paragraphs. Modern commentators have identified 282 laws, including property laws, commercial laws, and laws relating to marriage. The penalties mentioned range from fines and beatings to mutilation (such as the cutting off of a hand or putting out of an eye) and death. The punishments of imprisonment and forced labor were unknown.

The first few laws deal with legal procedures and the penalties for not following them correctly. For example, one law states that if a free man accuses another free man of murder but cannot prove guilt, the accuser himself will be put to death. Another law decrees that if a free man bears witness in a case and cannot prove his statement, the witness himself will be executed, but only if the case involves a matter of life and death.

Theft laws and family laws

Several laws deal with breaches of contract, property rights, and slaves. Some of the punishments for theft and burglary were very specific. For example, if a free man made a hole in a house with an intent to steal from it, he would be executed in front of that hole and then bricked in. If, on the other hand, a fire broke out in the house of a free man, and another free man entered to extinguish the fire but instead stole some of the inhabitant's possessions, the thief would be thrown into the fire and burned alive.

No less than 70 articles in the code deal with family law. The family was the basic unit of society. Sons had greater rights than daughters, however. For example, if only daughters were born to the parents, a son-in-law could take on all the functions of a son. It was acceptable to adopt a child, even though this practice was rare in other parts of the Semitic world. The adopted child might be an orphan or the child of a concubine or of relatives or friends.

Several other laws dealt with marriage (see box, page 70) and relations between the sexes. A sexual transgression could be harshly punished. If the wife of a free man was caught having sex with another man, both would be tied up, thrown into the Euphrates River, and left to drown.

Law and rank

The laws contained in Hammurabi's code did not apply equally to everyone. In Babylonian society, the people occupied different ranks, and their rights were determined by their status. At the top were the free people of the *awilu* class. These were the aristocrats, the wealthy, and the property owners, who probably lived in

The stele of King Hammurabi, from the 18th century BCE, is inscribed with his legal code, the first such code to survive in its entirety.

MARI

Mari was an ancient Semitic kingdom located on the upper Euphrates River in Syria at the intersection of a number of trade routes. As a pivotal center of trade, Mari had two eras of greatness, one during the first half of the third millennium BCE and another in the early part of the second millennium BCE. Its prosperity made it a rival to the Akkadian Empire of Sargon and the Babylonian Empire of Hammurabi. It was subdued by both of those powerful states.

The remains of Mari were discovered in 1933 CE by the French archaeologist André Parrot, who was excavating near Tell Hariri in Syria, close to the Iraqi border. His finds showed that the city had two golden ages. The first was ended when it was conquered by Sargon of Akkad, after which it was ruled first by Akkad, then by Ur, and finally by the emerging Ashur. It then had a short period of independence under its own dynasty; Zimrilim (ruled 1779–1757 BCE) was its most famous king. For a while, Zimrilim was an ally of Hammurabi. The kings exchanged cordial letters and sent ambassadors to each other's court. However, after conquering Larsa, Hammurabi turned on Mari around 1757 BCE, annexing it and destroying Zimrilim's capital city and palace.

The archaeological finds from the first period were sensational. A palace, a ziggurat, and a series of small temples, most of which were devoted to Semitic gods and goddesses, dated from that period. Two especially noteworthy temples were dedicated to Ishtar and Dagan. The style of the statues shows a marked Sumerian influence, suggesting that Mari had close contact with southern Mesopotamia at that time.

The palace of Zimrilim, dating from the second period, was a magnificent structure that must have been the envy of many contemporary kings. With more than 300 rooms, it measured 600 by 410 feet (183 by 125 m). The palace's rooms included royal apartments, offices, and store-rooms. The throne room was painted with striking murals, one of which showed Zimrilim being anointed as king by the goddess Ishtar.

This wall painting from a palace at Mari shows a sacrificial scene.

two-story brick houses with several rooms, in which the walls might be plastered. Next came a middle class of free people, called the *mushkenu*, who probably lived in smaller, single-story houses of mud brick.

At the bottom of the social hierarchy were the slaves, or *wardu*, who lived in poorer quarters. Most slaves were prisoners of war and were used by the king on public works programs, such as the construction of temples, roads, and irrigation canals. Others were people who had once been free but had been made slaves as the legal penalty for infractions of Hammurabi's code. Some slaves had been sold into slavery by their parents.

Slaves were considered to be property that could be bought and sold or used to pay debts. Under the code, whole families could be handed over to a creditor as slaves,

but only for a maximum of three years. Slaves were generally well treated (largely for economic reasons), and they also had some rights under the law. They were permitted to conduct business and even to borrow money and purchase their freedom.

Within this class structure, crime carried different penalties according to who had committed it and whom it was committed against. If a free man broke the leg of a nobleman, then his own leg would be broken as punishment. If he committed the same crime against a fellow member of the

This Babylonian statue from the 18th century BCE depicts a praying man. It is possible that the statue depicts King Hammurabi himself.

THE MARI LETTERS

When Mari was excavated in 1933 CE, an archive containing some 25,000 clay tablets was uncovered. The Mari Letters are made up of correspondence exchanged between the rulers of Mari and other kings and chieftains. As such, they provide a wealth of fascinating detail on the life of people in the central Euphrates region around 1800 BCE.

For example, a general wrote to the palace to complain that the auxiliaries he was expecting from the local communities were not forthcoming. He suggested that a criminal should be taken from prison and executed and that the criminal's head should be carried around the reluctant encampments, "so the soldiers will become afraid and will assemble here quickly."

Another letter from a son to his mother complained that he had only ragged clothes to wear even though "the clothes of young men are becoming more and more beautiful here…. [And even though the son of] a servant of my father has two new sets of clothes, you are already objecting to one new set for me!"

When Shamshi-Adad I (ruled 1813–1781 BCE) of Assyria was overlord of Mari, he appointed his son Yasmah-Adad as his viceroy there. However, the arrangement appears to have been far from satisfactory, and in a series of bitter letters, the father upbraids the son for his shortcomings, comparing him unfavorably with his more capable elder brother, who was a general of an army.

This depiction of people bringing goods as tribute is from Hammurabi's stele, which was created in the 18th century BCE.

middle class, the punishment would only be a fine of one silver mina. If he broke the leg of a slave, however, he would have to pay the slave's owner half of the slave's value in compensation.

Trade laws

There were various penalties for damage caused by neglect in various trades. For example, an architect who built a house that collapsed and killed the owner would be executed. Subsequent articles laid down the fixed rates payable for services rendered by trades. Workers in these trades were entitled to a minimum wage and to three days off each month. The code also laid down the maximum interest that could be charged for debt— not more than 33 percent was permitted for private debts.

Epilogue to the code

The code closes with an epilogue in praise of Hammurabi, who had been called by the gods to allow "the land to enjoy stable government and good rule." He wrote the laws on stone, he stated, so that "the strong may not oppress the weak, and that justice may be dealt to the orphan and the widow." He went on to say that he had inscribed his precious words on a stele and established it in Babylon before the statue of himself called the "King of Justice."

The epilogue ends with these words: "Let any oppressed man who has a cause come into the presence of my statue as king of justice, and let him have the inscription on my stele read out to him. Let him hear my precious words, so that my stele may make his rights clear to him, and let him know the law that applies to him, so that his heart may be set at ease."

Inherited gods

The gods of Babylonia were inherited from the Sumerians and Akkadians. The original head of this pantheon had been the deity Anu, god of the sky, but by the Babylonian period, his son, the god Enlil, the "Lord of the Winds," was considered to be the king of the gods. One of the most important female deities was Ishtar, the goddess of love and war. Known to the Sumerians as Inanna, she was identified with Venus, the evening star, and was often shown riding a lion, her sacred animal. From the Akkadians, the Babylonians adopted two other important gods—Shamash (the sun god) and Sin (the moon god). Two other deities of particular significance were the grain god Dagan and the weather god Adad, who was responsible for bringing rain.

Shamash had a particularly important role as the great judge, the "destroyer of evil" who watched over the Babylonians like a shepherd over his flock. He was thought to travel the skies daily in his chariot, seeing everything that happened on earth.

Creation and afterlife

One god who came to particular prominence during the reign of Hammurabi was Marduk. Marduk was important because of the role that he played in the Babylonian story of creation, which was told in an epic poem known as the *Enuma Elish*. The poem relates how Marduk defeated Tiamat, a primeval sea monster that was a symbol of chaos. From the body of this monster, Marduk made the earth and the heavens. The idea of a creator god creating order out of chaos was common in ancient societies. Marduk's victory over Tiamat was commemorated at every celebration of the Babylonian New Year and the *Enuma Elish* was recited at the festivals.

The Babylonians apparently believed in an afterlife. The souls of the dead were thought to journey to a netherworld and to continue life there in much the same way as on earth. For this reason, the dead were buried with the same tools, weapons, clothes, and jewelry that they had used on earth.

Another central aspect of Babylonian religion was the relationship of the gods

This relief depicts a musician playing a harp and dates to the early second millennium BCE.

These ancient stone walls are the remains of Hammurabi's palace in Babylon.

BABYLONIAN MARRIAGE CONTRACTS

Much of the Code of Hammurabi consists of laws dating back to ancient times, so the sections dealing with marriage often describe rules that had been in force in Mesopotamia for centuries. Family law allowed a man to have several wives, but he was only bound to one.

After the bride's parents had consented to the union, the marriage took place in a ceremony that consisted simply of witnessing the marriage contract. This agreement was inscribed on a clay tablet and defined the position of the two parties. The husband listed his conditions for accepting the woman as his wife, while the contract also contained a description of the woman's rights and duties. It spelled out the amount of money she would receive if she were to be rejected in the future and her punishment if she were to be unfaithful.

The marriage was also marked by the transfer of money or property from the bridegroom to his future father-in-law. After the marriage ceremony, these assets remained the possession of the bride's father. He in turn had to make a payment of a dowry, which remained the property of the wife. If the marriage was not completed because of a fault on the part of the groom, the bride's father would keep the money he had received. However, if the bride or her family defaulted so that the wedding did not take place, they had to pay back double the money they had received.

Under the old Sumerian law, a wife had various legal rights. She could be a witness to a contract; she could own property and administer it without reference to her husband; and she could engage independently in business. She was also entitled to the income from any assets she received from her husband. However, her husband could divorce her on very slender grounds, whereas it was much more difficult for her to divorce her husband.

in heaven with their representations on earth—their statues in the temples. The deity was thought to be present in his statue, so the statues were clothed, fed daily, and addressed as if they were living beings. The Babylonians believed they had been put on earth in order to serve the gods. For this reason, it was vitally important that they discovered the will of the gods.

Divination and astronomy

Various means were used to establish the thoughts of the gods. The priests who carried out such divination rituals were important people and were consulted by both high officials and ordinary citizens. The priests used a variety of means to determine the will of the gods, including studying the behavior of animals within the temple enclosure, observing the patterns of oil in water or smoke from incense, and studying the movements of heavenly bodies. Another type of divination involved the study of the internal organs of sacrificial animals; clay models of sheep livers bearing all kinds of inscriptions have been found in Mesopotamia.

Because the study of heavenly bodies was an important source of omens, a network of observatories was set up to study the stars and phenomena such as lightning, earthquakes, thunderstorms, and hail. These observatories collected astronomical data that is astonishingly accurate; the Babylonians have justly been called the fathers of astronomy.

This statue depicts King Ishtupilum, who was a ruler of Mari in the 18th century BCE. Mari was a powerful city-state that was a rival of Babylon.

The study of mathematics

The Babylonians developed a remarkably advanced mathematical system, based on the sexagesimal system of numbers (which uses sixty as a base number) that they had inherited from the Sumerians. Evidence collected from tablets intended for school use shows that they had multiplication and division tables, as well as tables for working out squares and square roots.

It is clear that Babylonian students of mathematics were taught how to solve geometric and algebraic problems and that much of the study was directed toward practical problems associated with engineering and quantity surveying. The Babylonians had standardized measures for weight, volume, length, and area, and their cuneiform writing had special combinations of signs to represent numbers, enabling elaborate calculations to be carried out.

Medicine

Ancient Babylonian texts indicate that doctors used various means to establish the cause of a patient's illness and the likelihood of recovery. The study of omens was an important part of the doctor's job; for example, the appearance of a particular type of animal in the vicinity of the patient was believed to indicate whether he or she would recover.

However, doctors also had more practical skills. They prescribed herbal remedies for specific illnesses and also sometimes carried out surgical operations. Mesopotamian doctors were skillful in setting broken bones. Surgery could be dangerous for both doctor and patient, however; doctors who accidentally injured people during surgical operations faced harsh punishments.

Fall of an empire

After the death of Hammurabi, the Babylonian Empire came under attack. Hammurabi's son Samsu-ilina (ruled 1749–1712 BCE) had to cope with rebellious cities in the south, while the Kassites from the east began making incursions into the weakening empire. By the end of Samsu-ilina's reign, the so-called Sealand dynasty was in control of southern Mesopotamia from the Persian Gulf to Nippur. For the next 100 years or so, Babylonia continued to lose both land and prestige to these enemy states. Around 1595 BCE, the Hittite king Mursilis I raided Babylon, sacking the city and seizing its wealth. In a symbolic act, he stole the statue of Marduk from the god's temple in the center of Babylon. The sacking of Babylon marked the end of Hammurabi's dynasty.

The next stage of Babylon's history is shrouded in mystery. It seems that the ruined state of Babylon was easy prey for its next conquerors, the kings of the Sealand dynasty, who controlled the city for a time. Then, around 1570 BCE, a Kassite king called Agum II seized power in Babylonia, soon controlling the area from the Euphrates to the Zagros Mountains. He is said to have recaptured the statue of Marduk and restored it to its temple, decking it out in a new set of clothes. This act would have made him popular with the Babylonians, and as the Kassite kings were also willing to adopt the customs, religion, and even the language of the conquered land, they soon became almost indistinguishable from earlier Mesopotamian rulers.

Kassite rule

The Kassite kings ruled Babylonia for the next four and a half centuries, during which time the city of Babylon once again became the administrative and cultural capital of a substantial Mesopotamian empire.

However, although the Kassites were successful in retaining power for a long time, they were constantly threatened by aggressive states menacing their borders. To the east, the Hurrians, who hailed from northwest Iran, were establishing a number of small states, while in the north, the kingdom of the Mittani was growing ever more powerful.

In the early 13th century BCE, the Kassites entered into a treaty of friendship with the Hittites. The pact was supposed to act as some kind of insurance against the growing might of Assyria. However, in 1225 BCE, Babylon was attacked and sacked by the Assyrian king Tukulti-Ninurta I, who massacred the city's inhabitants. Marduk's statue was

This piece of Assyrian metalwork from the eighth century BCE depicts a worshipper before the goddess Ishtar. Ishtar was worshipped by both the Babylonians and the Assyrians.

again carried off, this time to Assyria. This sacrilege was too much for the Babylonians, and even for some Assyrians, and in 1197 BCE, Tukulti-Ninurta was assassinated. The Kassite Babylonians regained their independence for a while, but in 1158 BCE, the Elamite king Shutruk-Nahhunte I sacked Babylon, deposed its king, and put an end to the Kassite dynasty.

The Second Dynasty of Isin

After a period of instability, a new royal line centered on the city of Isin emerged. This line was called the Second Dynasty of Isin, and its most famous king was Nebuchadnezzar I, who reigned from around 1125 to 1104 BCE. Nebuchadnezzar restored the morale of the Babylonians by inflicting a crushing defeat on the Elamites. Leading an army across the desert, he confronted the enemy before their capital, Susa. After his victory, he recovered the statue of Marduk, which Shutruk-Nahhunte had taken to Susa after the sack of Babylon.

During the next few centuries, Babylon was ruled by a succession of minor dynasties. This period was marked by numerous incursions of Aramaean tribesmen from the west who seized farming land wherever they could. Eventually, the Aramaeans managed to establish themselves permanently in the south, where they adapted to the local culture and became a major part of the population. However, the empire suffered from their plundering raids and many of the original Babylonians began to suffer from famine and poverty.

The New Empire

During the tenth and ninth centuries BCE, the Babylonians and Assyrians managed to coexist without too much friction, but in the eighth century BCE, a new foe appeared to disturb the political scene. The Chaldeans, a tribe of Semitic speakers, settled around the Persian Gulf. Unlike the seminomadic Aramaeans, the Chaldeans lived in prosperous villages, keeping cattle and horses and controlling the trade routes to the east. The Chaldean chiefs aspired to the Babylonian throne, and during the eighth century BCE, a Chaldean general

When rolled in wet clay, the Babylonian cylinder seal on the left would have created an imprint similar to that on the right. This particular seal, made in the 16th century BCE, depicts someone making an offering to a deity.

This reconstruction of Babylon's Ishtar Gate, made partially from the original tiles, stands in Berlin's Pergamon Museum. The original was constructed in the sixth century BCE.

named Merodach-baladan succeeded twice in briefly seizing the crown of Babylonia.

Defeat of the Assyrians

In 729 BCE, following the death of the Babylonian ruler Nabu-nasir, the Assyrian king Tiglath-pileser III led a campaign into Babylonia. After a series of military victories, he managed to establish Assyrian ascendancy over the region and make himself king of Babylonia. The Assyrians remained overlords of Babylon until 626 BCE, when a Chaldean general called Napolassar led a campaign of determined onslaughts aimed at ousting the Assyrians from the Babylonian plain.

Napolassar successfully managed to drive the Assyrians out. He then took the Babylonian crown for himself, restoring Babylonian independence from Assyria and ushering in the greatest period of Babylonian history.

The power of Assyria was on the wane, and Napolassar followed up his victory at home by joining forces with the Medes from the Iranian plain and attacking the Assyrians from two sides. Nineveh, the Assyrian capital, was taken in 612 BCE; three years later, the Assyrian Empire was totally destroyed. By this victory, Napolassar became king of a vast empire that stretched from the Mediterranean Sea to the Persian Gulf.

EPIC OF GILGAMESH

Many works of literature have survived from Babylonian times, the most famous of which is the *Epic of Gilgamesh*. This epic, inscribed in Akkadian cuneiform, was found on clay tablets among the remains of the library of the Assyrian king Ashurbanipal (ruled 668–627 BCE) when his capital, Nineveh, was being excavated in the 19th century CE. This epic dates from the time of Hammurabi and tells the story of Gilgamesh, a legendary king of Sumer whose character may have been based on that of one of the early rulers of Uruk.

As befits a legendary hero, Gilgamesh is immensely tall—11 feet (3.35 m)—and is two-thirds god and one-third human. He is described as striding "through the streets of Uruk like a wild ox, sublime of gait." Gilgamesh acquires a companion, a wild hairy man called Enkidu, who has proved the king's equal in a wrestling match. Together, the two heroes go forth into the world to perform great deeds. Their first adventure involves a trip to the forests of Lebanon, where they defeat the fearsome giant Chumbaba, king of the Cedar Mountain.

After more adventures, Enkidu falls ill and dies. Gilgamesh is heartbroken, and from then on, the story is no longer about an invincible hero and his glorious deeds; it is about a desperate, only-too-human Gilgamesh engaged in a bitter fight with death, the only enemy he cannot escape. Setting out on a search for immortality, Gilgamesh journeys to the "island of the blessed," where he eventually finds the herb of life deep in a spring. He picks the herb and starts on his return journey. Along the way, however, he goes swimming in a lake, leaving the precious herb of life on the shore, where it is eaten by a snake.

Robbed of his chance at immortality, Gilgamesh must settle for being mortal. However, he finds solace in contemplating his life's work. He built the walls of the great city of Uruk, and these walls are so strong that he predicts they will last for all eternity. So far, he has not been proved wrong.

This Assyrian relief sculpture from the eighth century BCE is believed to depict the hero Gilgamesh.

THE CITY OF BABYLON

The ancient city of Babylon lies on the Euphrates River in present-day Iraq, around 56 miles (90 km) south of Baghdad. Babylon was excavated between 1899 and 1913 CE by a German archaeological team led by Robert Koldewey, who uncovered the city as it had been in its final years, in the reign of Nebuchadnezzar II. The city was built on either side of the Euphrates, which flowed though its middle. Babylon covered an area of 2,100 acres (850 ha) and was home to a quarter of a million people, making it larger than many modern towns.

Babylon was rectangular in shape and was surrounded by two mighty walls. These walls were so thick that, according to the Greek historian Herodotus, it was possible for two chariots to be driven side by side along the top of each wall. The walls were pierced by nine great gates made of bronze. The most magnificent of them was the Ishtar Gate, which was covered with yellow and blue tiles that incorporated reliefs of lions and bulls, symbols of the gods Ishtar and Adad. Reconstructions of this gate can be seen in Baghdad and Berlin.

Inside the city walls were the palace of Nebuchadnezzar, the Esagila (the main temple of Marduk, the patron god of Babylon), and houses for the citizens. The temple was connected to the Ishtar Gate by a wide avenue called the Processional Way. During the annual New Year festivities, the king led a procession in which the statue of Marduk was carried through the Ishtar Gate to temples outside the city. North of Marduk's temple stood the ziggurat of Babylon, called the Etemenanki or "House of the Foundation of Heaven and Earth." It had seven stories and rose to a height of 300 feet (91 m). Many commentators have identified this ziggurat with the Tower of Babel in the Bible.

Nebuchadnezzar II

The taking of Nineveh marked the beginning of the Neo-Babylonian Empire. In 605 BCE, Napolassar's son Nebuchadnezzar led a campaign against the Egyptians, who had marched into Syria as far as Carchemish on the upper Euphrates River. He achieved a magnificent victory, but on the same day, he received news of his father's death. Hurrying back to Babylon, he ascended the throne as Nebuchadnezzar II, beginning one of the most brilliant reigns in the history of Babylon.

Nebuchadnezzar followed up his triumph at Carchemish by conquering Syria, Phoenicia, and Judah, where Jerusalem fell to him in 597 BCE. Several years later, Jerusalem rebelled, but after a siege, the Babylonians took it again. Nebuchadnezzar exacted a terrible revenge on the inhabitants of Jerusalem. The rebellious governor was forced to watch while his sons were killed in front of him. He was then blinded and taken in chains to Babylon. Jerusalem was put to the torch, its leaders were executed, and most of its inhabitants were deported to Babylonia. Because of his destruction of Jerusalem, Nebuchadnezzar is a key figure in the Old Testament of the Bible, where his exploits are described in the Book of Daniel.

The Hanging Gardens

Nebuchadnezzar is chiefly remembered today for inaugurating a great building program in Babylon. Attempting to rebuild the empire of Hammurabi, he restored old temples and constructed new buildings throughout Babylonia. He rebuilt Babylon, enlarging it and making it far more splendid than it had ever been. He also embellished it with the famous Hanging Gardens, one of the seven wonders of the world. The gardens were reputedly built as a gift for his wife, a Median princess named Amyitis, so she would not miss the landscape of her homeland. The Hanging Gardens were famous in the ancient world and were mentioned in the works of several later Greek writers, including Strabo and Diodorus Siculus. However, present-day archaeological excavations have been unable to locate the gardens.

After Nebuchadnezzar's death in 562 BCE, revival efforts were lost in a series of power struggles. In 556 BCE, an elderly general named Nabonidus took the throne. He is a mysterious figure. Only three years into his reign, he left Babylon in the care of his son Belshazzar and went to live in Teiman in the Arabian Desert. Ten years later, he returned to Babylon, but his reign was doomed. In 539 BCE, Cyrus, king of Persia, invaded Babylonia. Nabonidus fled, but he and his son were both captured and killed. The Persians captured Babylon without resistance. Babylonia was annexed, becoming a province of the Persian Empire. Its days as an independent realm were at an end.

See also:

The Assyrians (page 102) • The Hittites (page 78) • The Persians (page 126) • The Sumerians (page 46)

The Hanging Gardens of Babylon, depicted here in an 18th-century-CE engraving, are believed to have been built by King Nebuchadnezzar II to ease the homesickness of his bride.

THE HITTITES

In the second millennium BCE, a tribe of formidable warriors based in Anatolia (present-day Turkey) built an empire that was to rival those of ancient Babylon and Egypt and last for 500 years. They were known as the Hittites.

The Hittites were a group of Indo-European peoples who migrated from central Asia some time around 2000 BCE. They conquered an area of Anatolia called Hatti, from which they got their name. The region was to become the center of a vast empire that stretched deep into Syria to the south. The Hittites flourished from around 1700 to 1200 BCE and were one of the major powers of western Asia.

In Assyrian and Egyptian sculptures, the Hittites are portrayed as powerful-looking men with flat foreheads, slanted eyes, and hair in braids hanging down their backs. They vaguely resemble later Turks and Mongols. However, in other sculptures, the Hittites are pictured with different features, leading some historians to conclude that they came from a mixture of races.

Hattushash

The center of the Hittites' domain was the mountainous central region of Anatolia, and their capital was the great city of Hattushash (see box, page 82), set in a natural fortress position in the north of this region. The history of the Hittites begins around 1850 BCE, when a prince called Anittas set out to extend his small kingdom in central Anatolia by conquering the cities of Kanesh and Hattushash. Although Hattushash was located in a commanding position, Anittas destroyed it completely and declared its ground to be cursed. Several generations later, another king, called Labarnas, decided to rebuild Hattushash and make it his capital. To commemorate the event, Labarnas changed his name to Hattusilis (meaning "man of Hattushash").

It was this king, Hattusilis I (ruled c. 1650–1620 BCE), who was the real founder of the Hittite Empire. He was eager to conquer new territory, and after consolidating his position in central Anatolia he marched his army south across the Taurus Mountains to the Mediterranean Sea. Turning east, he invaded northern Syria, a region that was then ruled by the kings of a city called Aleppo. From Syria, Hattusilis brought back a band of scribes, whose task was to teach cuneiform writing to the Hittites.

Hattusilis was succeeded by his grandson, Mursilis I, who was equally imperialist in his mind-set. First, Mursilis conquered Aleppo. Then, marching east along the Euphrates River, he invaded Mesopotamia, sacking Babylon in 1595 BCE. However, while the Hittite army was returning home, it was attacked by the Hurrians, an aggressive tribe based

This sculpture depicts a Hittite god. In art, Hittite gods were often shown wearing horned helmets.

on the upper Euphrates River. The Hittite army was routed, and when Mursilis finally managed to reach home, he was murdered by his brother-in-law. While conflicts within the royal family escalated, this first Hittite Empire went into rapid decline.

This statue depicts Tarunza, a Hittite king who ruled the city of Malatya.

The New Kingdom

The next major chapter in Hittite history began in the early 14th century BCE, when King Suppiluliumas I (ruled c. 1358–1323 BCE) founded the New Kingdom. Suppiluliumas dedicated himself to restoring the fortunes of the Hittites and began by reconquering the territories in southern Anatolia that had previously been Hittite possessions. He then advanced into Syria, where he conquered several city-states, reaching as far south as Damascus. Turning east, Suppiluliumas sought to subdue the Hurrians and defeated them at the Battle of Carchemish. He then turned the Hurrians' kingdom into a vassal state by installing a minor Hurrian prince on the throne, making him swear loyalty to the Hittites, and marrying him to a Hittite princess.

Suppiluliumas also turned the conquered Syrian cities into vassals. By doing so, he built up an empire of confederate states that owed allegiance to the Hittites. They were bound by treaty to pay a substantial annual tribute to their masters. At the same time, they supplied a number of soldiers to the Hittite army. Suppiluliumas's success in expanding his empire depended both on the efficient organization of his new Hittite state, which was run along strictly military lines, and on his extremely formidable army (see box, page 85).

Suppiluliumas's successors were equally dedicated to maintaining and expanding the Hittite Empire. They waged war against neighboring tribes and took on the might of Egypt, which was trying to halt the Hittite expansion. Suppiluliumas's son, Mursilis II, fought the mountain tribes to the north and succeeded in extending Hittite domination westward to the Aegean coast. There he created a series of vassal states. To protect his kingdom from attacks from the north, Mursilis built a line of

THE HITTITE EMPIRE

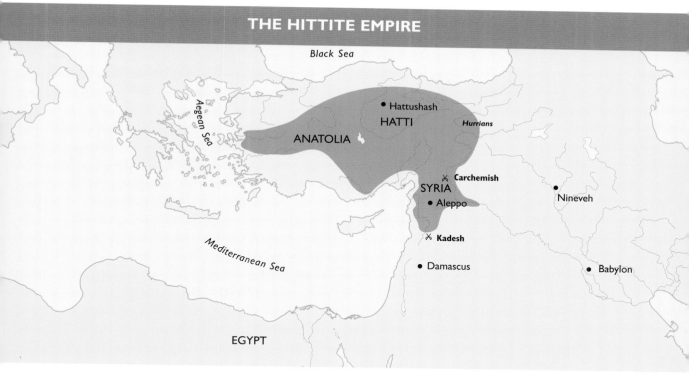

Black Sea

Aegean Sea

• Hattushash

HATTI

ANATOLIA

Hurrians

⚔ **Carchemish**

SYRIA

• **Aleppo**

• Nineveh

Mediterranean Sea

⚔ **Kadesh**

• Damascus

• Babylon

EGYPT

KEY

Extent of Hittite
Empire in 1400
BCE

⚔ Major battle

fortresses that were permanently garrisoned by soldiers.

Despite Mursilis's efforts, the kingdom came under renewed attack from northern tribes during the reign of his successor, Muwatallis. The end result of these attacks was the destruction of Hattushash. In response, Muwatallis moved his capital city farther south. He also subdued the vassal states of Arzawa in the west, which were in revolt.

The Battle of Kadesh

Having resecured the loyalty of the Arzawa states, Muwatallis went to war with Egypt, which was then under the rule the Pharaoh Ramses II. Ramses was anxious to retake the Hittite cities in Syria that had formerly been under Egyptian control. In 1275 BCE, Muwatallis assembled an enormous army and lay in wait for the Egyptians behind the city of Kadesh. As the Egyptians entered the city from the south, the Hittite army took

them by surprise. What followed was one of the greatest battles of ancient history, which is said to have involved around 5,000 chariots. Initially, the Hittites had the upper hand, but the late arrival of reinforcements helped the Egyptians drive their enemies back. Ramses claimed victory, but it seems more likely that the battle ended in a stalemate. In any case, the Hittites remained in control of Syria.

Hattusilis III (ruled c. 1275–1250 BCE) concluded peace treaties with both Egypt and Babylon. The treaty with Egypt was sealed by the marriage of a Hittite princess to Ramses. For a time, the Hittite Empire enjoyed an unparalleled period of peace and prosperity, but in the second half of the 13th century, it was threatened by the growing power of the Assyrian Empire to the east. In the west, meanwhile, warrior races known as the Sea Peoples were threatening the coast of Anatolia. It is thought that thee

81

HATTUSHASH

Hattushash, the capital of the Hittite Empire, was founded by King Hattusilis I around 1650 BCE. Its ruins lie in central Turkey, close to a present-day village called Bogazkoy. Hattushash was built on a high, rocky ridge, making it a natural fortress. Because much of the ground was sloping, earth terraces were constructed to provide flat ground on which to build houses.

The city covered an area of around 400 acres (162 ha) and was encircled by a massive rampart 4 miles (6 km) long. This encircling fortification consisted of a great earthen embankment surmounted by a stone wall with towers and battlements. The gates that led into the city were decorated with large relief sculptures carved into stone—twin sphinxes at the Sphinx Gate, two ferocious lions at the Lion Gate, and a young soldier complete with battle-ax at the King's Gate.

The city was carefully planned, with streets as straight as the land allowed. A drainage channel ran down the center of the bigger streets, covered over with large slabs of stone. This channel received dirty water from the houses on either side, through a system of smaller pipes.

The houses in Hattushash were constructed on stone foundations, with walls of sun-dried mud bricks. Flat roofs made of mud and brushwood were laid over wooden beams. There were few windows, so the houses were very dark inside. The floors were made of either flagstone or beaten earth, and most houses had a hearth for a fire and an oven. Some houses had a stone sink connected to the drain, and clay baths have also been found. There was little furniture, so most people ate their meals and slept on the floor.

In the Lower Town (in the northern part of the city), there was a great temple set in an enormous enclosure, roughly square shaped,

The ruins of the Hittite capital at Hattushash. The city was the center of the Hittite Empire from around 1650 to 1190 BCE.

measuring about 900 feet (275 m) on each side. This area was surrounded by a precinct wall that in part coincided with the wall of the lower city. On the eastern side of the city, towering over the Lower Town, stood the citadel, on which was built a magnificent palace with pillared walkways for the king. Although all the buildings have long been destroyed, it is thought that the palace contained several courtyards, around which were grouped the royal residences and a large audience hall.

At its height, Hattushash was a bustling city, the center of a great empire. It would have been an important market place for local farmers and for traveling merchants selling their wares. The city contained many taverns, eating houses, granaries, and craftsmen's workshops, and the streets would have been thronged with thousands of people going about their business.

Sea Peoples probably overran Anatolia around 1190 BCE, sacking Hattushash (once again the capital city) and destroying the Hittite Empire.

The Neo-Hittites

In Syria, the cities that had been conquered by the Hittites retained a Hittite identity for the following five centuries. In this so-called Neo-Hittite kingdom, the most important town was Carchemish. Situated alongside one of the three fords across the Euphrates River, Carchemish was well placed to dominate the major trade route from Nineveh to the Mediterranean Sea. Carchemish was also almost impregnable. Although it was often attacked, the town remained unconquered until it succumbed to the Assyrian king Sargon II in 717 BCE.

Hittite society

The king was at the top of Hittite society, combining the roles of military commander, supreme ruler, chief priest, and highest judge. He was supported by nobles and officials who were generally members of his own family. In order to secure the loyalty of the cities and provinces throughout the empire, the king would usually put the local governments in the hands of his family members or arrange a royal marriage to achieve the same ends.

The society was feudal, meaning that the nobles and provincial vassals each had to swear a personal oath of loyalty to the king. In return, the nobles held large tracts of land, each with its own retainers, such as peasants and artisans, who in turn had to swear loyalty to their lord. The

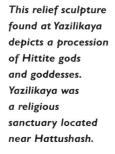

This relief sculpture found at Yazilikaya depicts a procession of Hittite gods and goddesses. Yazilikaya was a religious sanctuary located near Hattushash.

retainers also had to pay annual dues, either in goods or services, such as working on the lord's land or doing military service.

Most of the Hittite people were peasant farmers who worked on the land, growing wheat and barley, along with peas and onions. They also cultivated apple, fig, and olive trees, as well as grape vines. Wool, meat, and milk were provided by herds of sheep, pigs, and cattle.

Crafts

Skilled artisans and craftspeople made up an important section of Hittite society. There were stonemasons, carpenters, potters, and metalsmiths. Doctors, tailors, cobblers, bakers, merchants, and innkeepers could also be found in the cities.

Hittite metalworkers were highly skilled in both bronze working and, from around 1700 BCE, the technique of iron smelting. In most parts of the world, the Iron Age had not yet begun and the pioneering art of smelting was a closely guarded secret. Local mines provided ingots of raw iron ore, which were transported to refineries where they were heated to high temperatures to extract iron. Iron was used to make tools and weapons, but because it was scarce, most weapons were still made of bronze. Silver, used as a medium of exchange, was mined in the Taurus Mountains, where there was an abundance of the metal.

The Hittites wore woolen clothes, woven from yarn spun at home. Men wore a long-sleeve, knee-length tunic, usually belted at the waist and fastened with bronze pins at the shoulders. Another longer tunic, known as a Hurrian shirt, was reserved for special occasions such as festivals and was embroidered or decorated with bronze ornaments. Women wore lighter clothes, with a long woolen cloak for outdoors. Both men and women wore their hair long, sometimes in a pigtail, and both sexes wore jewelry such as necklaces, bracelets, rings, and earrings.

Hittite art

The most important period of Hittite artistic development lasted from 1450 to 1200 BCE and drew on earlier sources

This sanctuary at Eflatun Pinar was a place of worship during the time of the Hittite Empire.

THE HITTITE ARMY

To achieve their imperialistic aims, the Hittite kings needed an efficient fighting force. A small permanent troop of infantry served as the king's bodyguard and also carried out other duties such as patrolling the empire's frontiers. However, when the king embarked on a military campaign, a much larger force, numbering up to 30,000 men, was needed.

The soldiers were recruited from the estates of the Hittite nobles or from satellite kingdoms. Sometimes their numbers were augmented by mercenaries. The army consisted of two main divisions—foot soldiers and charioteers. The charioteers were highly skilled. The horse-drawn chariots were built of timber and were lightweight, fast, and exceptionally maneuverable. However, the chariots were also easily overturned, so a steady nerve and a sure hand were needed to keep them upright in a charge. Each chariot carried three men—a charioteer to drive the chariot, a warrior with a spear, and a soldier with a shield to protect the other two.

Following behind the chariots came the infantry, which were armed with daggers, long spears, and sickle-shaped swords that were used with a slashing movement. Some soldiers also used axes and bows and arrows. For protection in battle, the soldiers wore pointed helmets, with hanging flaps that covered the cheeks and neck. Sometimes, the foot soldiers wore body armor made of small overlapping scales of bronze, covered by a leather tunic, and carried shields to ward off blows.

As supreme military commander, the king generally led his army into battle himself. Lesser commands were held by members of the nobility. The army was divided into units of 10, 100, and 1,000 men. All units were subjected to rigorous training that resulted in a highly disciplined and efficient fighting force, which meant that troops could be moved quickly and secretly into position to make a surprise attack.

It is not known how the soldiers were paid. A large army was expensive to maintain, and it is probable that the troops lived by plundering the local inhabitants when in enemy territory. After a success in battle, booty was distributed liberally, which gave the army an extra incentive to be on the victorious side.

This statue depicts a Hittite soldier, wearing the pointed helmet that was typically used by Hittite troops at the time of the empire.

from Sumer and Babylon, as well as local Anatolian influences from the third millennium BCE. Hittite metalworkers produced elaborate bronze and gold ornaments, while Hittite potters produced jugs, cups, and vases, sometimes modeled in the shape of animals or birds. The Hittites were skilled at carving. Some particularly impressive representations of their deities were found at Carchemish. Made to adorn a royal robe, these ornaments were carved in lapis lazuli and mounted on gold.

Stonemasons made giant stone relief sculptures of animals, humans, and gods. In one great sanctuary, a magnificent series of mythological scenes, discovered carved

in rock, depicts lions and sphinxes serving gods and goddesses. Other carvings have shown gods wearing high pointed hats, short-skirted robes, and boots with long curling toes, clothes that identify them as part of the pantheon of Mesopotamian and northern Syrian gods adopted by the Hittites.

Reliefs at Carchemish suggest that music and dancing were popular with the later Hittites. One relief depicts soldiers

This gravestone depicts a Hittite nobleman and his wife from Marash, which was an important Hittite city.

VILLAGE LIFE

Most people in Hittite society did not live in a town or city but in small village communities that were largely self-sufficient. Each village had its own area of agricultural land, which was separated from the land of other nearby villages by tracts of fallow land. The villagers grew their crops and pastured their animals on the land belonging to their village, most of which was held in common.

Some of the inhabitants of a village might not be native Hittites but people who had been relocated from conquered regions. These new arrivals were settled on Hittite land and helped to increase the productivity of the village. There would also be some craftsmen living in the village, and they might hold individual plots of land on lease. In addition to their services as crafts-

men, they were required to spend time working on community projects such as digging irrigation channels and sinking wells.

Village life was governed by a body of senior members of the community, or elders. The elders were responsible for maintaining law and order in the village and for protecting any strangers who arrived on village land. An elder was usually the head of a household and as such had the power to give his daughters away in marriage.

As well as producing enough food to feed themselves, the villagers had to pay regular taxes to the central government. Native-born Hittite citizens also had to serve a term of military duty when required.

dancing, wearing animal skins and hiding their faces behind masks. Other reliefs show more scenes from day-to-day life, such as the king speaking to his vizier, with his hand resting on the vizier's shoulder, and a queen carrying a small prince on her arm, with the prince leading a tame ox by a rope.

Religion

The Hittites originally tended to worship a local god, and their prayers were primarily directed at securing favorable weather to ensure a good harvest. As the empire became unified, a centralized form of religion developed, incorporating a large number of deities. As chief priest, it became the duty of the king to travel around the country and preside over important religious festivals. It was believed that if a king neglected this duty, perhaps because he was away on a military campaign, the gods would become angry and the state would suffer. Mursilis II was noted for his pious observance of his priestly duties, and several of his prayers have survived. In one prayer, he begged the gods to intercede to save people from a dreadful plague that was ravaging the nation.

Archives found at Hattushash give many details about the large pantheon of deities worshipped in the Old Hittite period, together with descriptions of the ceremonies and hymns of the various religious cults. Texts relating ancient myths also clarify the complex nature of the cults, some of which seem to have been derived and adapted from other cultures. A common theme in many of the myths is one of order and chaos, and the related battles of the gods.

Many myths of the Old Hittite period feature storm gods and sun deities.

Some myths appear to have been derived from older traditional Hatti ones. One story tells of a battle between a storm god and the serpent monster Illuyanka. In the later empire period, other myths were adopted from the conquered Hurrians. Some stories involved Teshup, the storm god, who was to become the head of the Hittite pantheon of deities. Teshup was often accompanied by his consort Arinna, the sun goddess. A powerful rival of Teshup was Kumarbi, the god of grain and the harvest. Some deities were also adopted from the Mesopotamian and Syrian religions, including Ishtar, the goddess of war, who was called Shauska by the Hittites.

Lions were popular subjects for Hittite sculptors. This is one of several surviving statues of the animal.

THE DISAPPEARING GOD

Among the many myths that told stories of the gods of the Hittites was the one of the disappearing god. This story had several versions, but in all of them a god withdraws from the world, either in a fit of anger or because he wants to indulge himself in a pleasurable pursuit, such as hunting.

In one version, Telepinu, the god of fertility and agriculture, became annoyed with the world, lost his temper, and vanished. In doing so, he caused all life on earth to shrivel up and die. In another version, it was the sun god that disappeared, leaving the world to succumb to cold and frost. In all versions of the story, the other gods frantically search without success for the god that is missing. One account tells how the goddess Hannahanna (meaning "grandmother") has the idea of sending a bee to find the god. The bee has no difficulty in locating the god, and once it has found him, it stings him. The bee then puts wax over the sting to stop the pain and guides the errant god back to the others. When the disappearing god has returned, the world begins to thrive once more.

Nature deities, particularly those of mountains, rivers, and springs, were worshipped by the Hittites.

One of the most important religious sites for the Hittites was the ravine sanctuary at Yazilikaya. A relief carved in rock at the sanctuary shows a procession of 70 gods and goddesses, some of which are standing on the backs of animals sacred to them. The procession is led by Teshup. In the reliefs, many of the storm gods look very similar. They are shown wearing short kilts with wide belts and tall helmets with horns, and they are holding swords and battle-axes. In their priestly role, kings are shown dressed in caps and long robes and holding a long curved staff, the symbol of a priest. The king is sometimes shown standing before a sacrificial altar and at other times being embraced by a god.

This Hittite altar dates to around 1450 BCE.

Language and writing

It is thought that the Hittites spoke an Indo-European language, probably brought to Anatolia by waves of Indo-European settlers toward the end of the third millennium BCE. The Indo-European languages were derived from Sanskrit, an ancient Indian language, and were to become the basis of Greek and Latin, giving rise to all the modern European languages. Several ancient Hittite words bear a remarkable resemblance to their present-day English equivalents. For example, the Hittite word for "daughter" was *dohter*, while "water" was *watar*.

The Hittites used two writing systems—hieroglyphs (picture writing) and the wedge-shaped signs of the cuneiform script. The hieroglyphic script consisted of signs representing certain ideas, such as king, city, and god, together with other signs representing sounds. The lines of script were read

Cuneiform tablets such as this were used to keep records of transactions as well as to record history. Thousands of Hittite tablets have been found.

alternately from right to left and from left to right, in the same way that a plow makes furrows in the earth.

When the city of Hattushash was excavated in the early 20th century CE, around 20,000 clay tablets of cuneiform writing were found. Historians believe the tablets, which were written in both Akkadian (the international language of diplomacy at the time) and Hittite itself, make up the royal archives. In the years immediately following the tablets' discovery, the Czech scholar Bedrich Hrozny succeeded in deciphering the cuneiform texts, making the Hittite language accessible to modern scholars. He also revealed a history of the Hittite civilization that had been lost for more than 3,000 years.

See also:

The Assyrians (page 102) • Egypt's Middle Kingdom (page 14)

THE HITTITE LEGAL CODE

A collection of around 200 laws found at Hattushash has provided a remarkable insight into the Hittite legal code. The laws were inscribed on tablets probably around 1500 BCE. The code was one of the most lenient codes of antiquity, being based on restitution rather than retribution. Whereas most other societies used death or mutilation to punish wrongdoing, the Hittites moved toward more humane types of punishment.

Early statutes recorded on the tablets did indeed prescribe death—by drawing and quartering—for a range of crimes including rape and, for slaves, disobedience and black magic. In the case of other crimes, the offender's nose and ears might be cut off. A murder committed outside the city attracted a more severe punishment than one committed inside the city walls—because, it was said, in the countryside there was less chance of the victim's cries for help being heard. However, despite these early harsh punishments, it soon became possible for convicted criminals to substitute an animal to receive the penalty on their behalf, and for murder or theft, the criminals could pay an amount of money in compensation.

The code also provides information about Hittite marriage customs. At a wedding among aristocratic landowners, the husband would give his bride a large dowry, which was kept by the bride's parents. If the couple later divorced, the dowry had to be returned to the husband. If the husband died, his brother had to marry the widow, even if he already had a wife.

THE PHOENICIANS

The Phoenicians were a seafaring people who built up a vast trading network around the Mediterranean Sea in the third and second millenniums BCE. They were also responsible for creating one of the world's earliest alphabets.

By the beginning of the first millennium BCE, the Phoenicians were renowned as intrepid seafarers and astute traders throughout the Mediterranean area. From their base on the shores of the eastern Mediterranean, they set up trading posts throughout the region, becoming the carriers of the Mediterranean world. They also provided a vital link to the caravans that brought exotic merchandise from the east.

No one is sure where the Phoenicians originally came from, but they were probably settled in what is now Syria, Lebanon, and Israel by around 3000 BCE. In their own language, they called themselves Canaanites, which suggests they may have been descended from the original inhabitants of the land of Canaan (present-day Palestine). In the Semitic language, however, *Canaan* also means "the land of purple," so the name may be unconnected to their geographical origins and refer merely to the purple dye for which the Phoenicians were famous.

The Phoenicians occupied a narrow strip of land around 260 miles (418 km) northeast of Egypt that consisted of the coastal area of today's Lebanon, together with parts of modern Israel and Syria. Bordered by the Lebanon Mountains to the east, this fertile area was around 200 miles (321 km) long and around 30 miles (48 km) wide. From this small base, the Phoenicians eventually dominated trade throughout the Mediterranean region.

Early history

Between 3000 and 2000 BCE, the Phoenicians built several cities, including Ugarit and Byblos. By around 2600 BCE, the Phoenicians were trading with merchants in Egypt. There is a record of an Egyptian expedition to the Phoenician port of Byblos around this time to buy 40 shiploads of cedar wood.

By 1500 BCE, the Phoenician ports had become thriving trading centers, but the second half of the millennium was to see the Phoenicians lose their independence to a succession of foreign invaders, including the Egyptians, the Hittites, and the Mycenaeans. Around 1100 BCE, however, the Phoenicians were able to throw off foreign domination and to emerge as the dominant sea power of the Mediterranean region.

Phoenicia wielded an influence far beyond its size. Its great cities of Arvad, Byblos, Ugarit, Berytus, Sidon, and Tyre were hubs of international trade. These cities set up trading stations and colonies in Sicily and Cyprus, and as far away as Gades (present-day Cadiz) in Spain. In 814 BCE, the city of Tyre established a colony called Carthage on the north coast of Africa. Carthage would become the most powerful Phoenician city of all.

Independent kingdoms

Phoenicia was not one united kingdom; it operated as a loose confederation of city-states. Each city had its own king, who came from a royal family that claimed divine descent, which meant that the king could only be chosen from that family. The king ruled with the help of a council of elders chosen from the most powerful merchant families. These elders appointed magistrates who were entrusted with the administration of daily government.

The greatest of the city-states was Tyre (meaning "rock"), which was actually made up of two distinct parts—an

This terra-cotta mask was made by Phoenician craftsmen around the seventh century BCE.

91

offshore island and a town on the nearby mainland. The island had two harbors, along with a number of closely packed houses, some of which were several stories high, built on the rocks. Into these houses was crammed a teaming population of timber merchants, shipbuilders, sailors, weavers, and cloth dyers.

Trading in timber

One of Phoenicia's most valuable resources was timber. The region's mountains were covered in forests of Lebanon cedars, trees that were valuable for the exceptionally hard timber they yielded. The Phoenicians built their own ships out of this material but also exported a great deal, particularly to Egypt, which had no trees of its own apart from palm trees.

The rot-resistant qualities of the cedar wood made it especially valuable for shipbuilding, and ancient historical records show that the Egyptian pharaohs used Phoenician wood for both their private boats and their holy ships. Around 950 BCE, King Solomon of Israel imported Lebanon cedar to use as the beams for his temple in Jerusalem. He also recruited Phoenician carpenters and construction workers to handle the project because, according to the Bible, nobody could work with wood as well as the Sidonians, as the Israelites called the Phoenicians.

Another important export was cloth, particularly the purple-dyed cloth used by royalty (see box, page 96), while glassworkers made highly prized glass vessels from the fine white sand found on Phoenicia's shores (see box, page 94). Phoenician craftsmen also worked with imported metals and other raw materials to produce finely wrought jewelry and tools for export. Delicate, decorative panels were carved from African ivory and used to embellish furniture produced by Phoenician carpenters.

Lords of the sea

In the early part of the first millennium BCE, the Phoenicians were the preeminent sailors in the Mediterranean region. While this status was partly due to their seamanship, the quality of their ships was also an important factor. Phoenician ships had a wide, flat hull to hold plenty of cargo, while a double deck offered space for two rows of oarsmen. With a square sail on a single mast, these ships were fast and highly maneuverable. They enabled the Phoenicians to criss-cross the Mediterranean and even venture into the Atlantic and Indian oceans.

The Phoenicians were first and foremost traders. As well as importing goods and exporting their own raw materials and products, the Phoenicians acted as

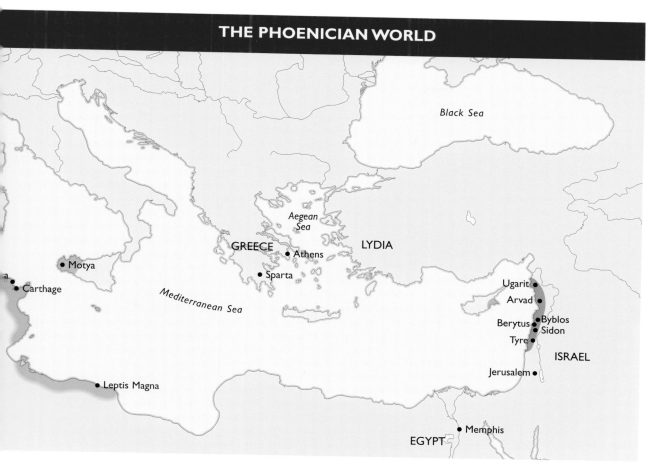

THE PHOENICIAN WORLD

Black Sea

Aegean Sea

GREECE   LYDIA

• Athens

• Sparta

Mediterranean Sea

• Motya

• Carthage

• Leptis Magna

Ugarit •
Arvad •
Berytus • • Byblos
• Sidon
Tyre •

ISRAEL

Jerusalem •

• Memphis

EGYPT

wholesalers, retailers, and transporters of goods. Phoenicia was ideally situated for trade, lying between the prosperous Egyptians to the south and the Hittites to the northwest and on the main caravan routes that brought goods from Mesopotamia and the east to the Mediterranean and northern Africa. Although they were known primarily as seafaring merchants, the Phoenicians did not conduct their trade exclusively by sea; they carried goods by land as far as Babylon in present-day Iraq.

The Phoenicians established good relations with the major powers of the eastern Mediterranean. In 950 BCE, Israel's King Solomon entered into a trade agreement with King Hiram of Tyre to do business with the people

living on the coast of the Red Sea. This arrangement probably extended to the people of western Arabia and beyond—the land of Ophir in the Bible. The pharaohs of Egypt employed Phoenicians to help build and sail fleets, and to equip expeditions. The Egyptians even allowed Phoenicia to establish a trading post at Memphis, in the heart of commercial Egypt.

Carthage and other colonies

At a great many strategic points along the Mediterranean coastline, the Phoenicians owned warehouses and trading posts. Over the years, some of these posts developed into large colonies and cities, the most famous of which is Carthage (in present-day Tunisia).

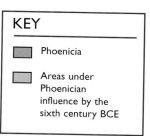

KEY

▨ Phoenicia

▨ Areas under Phoenician influence by the sixth century BCE

93

Carthage was founded in 814 BCE by a group of discontented or exiled citizens of Tyre, who had been forced to leave their country for political reasons. They sailed to the African coast and landed near Utica, one of Tyre's colonies. At that landing spot, they founded a new colony called Qart-hadasht (meaning "new city"), later known as Carchédon to the Greeks and Carthage to the Romans. There are several mythical versions of the story about the founding of this city. The most famous version is in Virgil's *Aeneid*, where the city is founded by Queen Dido, a fugitive from Tyre who becomes the lover of the Trojan hero Aeneas.

Carthage was located on a large bay and enjoyed a natural harbor—one of the best in the Mediterranean. The site could be easily defended and was perfectly situated for overseas trade. In the centuries following its foundation, Carthage grew into a rich and powerful city, trading in goods and materials such as textiles, pottery, and silver mined in Africa and Spain. Carthage continued to flourish until it was eventually destroyed by Roman forces in 146 BCE.

The Phoenicians had a knack for finding strategic places. They founded a colony at Massilia (present-day Marseilles) long before the Greeks. They also founded a number of settlements in Spain; Phoenician colonies at Gades and present-day Barcelona, Málaga, and Algeciras were important because of Spain's abundance of copper and silver.

Gades was the last stop before Phoenician ships sailed out into the Atlantic on what was one of their longest and most demanding voyages—a trading expedition to a place that the Phoenicians called the Tin Islands. This destination was actually the British Isles, where tin was mined in the extreme southwest (present-day Cornwall). The Phoenicians mixed the tin with copper to make bronze.

Navigation and exploration

Voyages beyond the confines of the Mediterranean were only possible because of the Phoenicians' superior seamanship and navigating abilities. On every voyage, the Phoenician captains made careful observation of shores, distances, landmarks, currents, and wind direction. By doing so, they built up a wealth of precise navigational knowledge. They are also believed to have been the first sailors to use the Pole Star (Polaris) as an aid to navigation. Because of the lucrative nature of their business,

PHOENICIAN GLASSWARE

The white sand that lined the shores of Phoenicia was the source of silica, which, with wood ash, was an essential ingredient for the transparent glass that provided the Phoenicians with an important export. The Phoenician glassworkers were highly skilled in glassmaking and in producing beautifully decorated glassware. Although the Phoenicians may have invented glassblowing, most of their glassware was produced by a simpler technique called the sand-core method.

For this technique, the craftsman made a mold of sand in the required shape and then poured molten glass over the mold. When the glass coating had cooled and set, the sand was emptied out, leaving a hollow glass vessel. Patterns of different colored glass were then dripped on to the vessel, which was then rolled on a flat surface to set the pattern before the glass cooled. The result would be an elegant piece of highly decorative glassware that was prized throughout the Mediterranean region.

This stone relief from the palace of the Assyrian king Sargon II depicts wood being unloaded from Phoenician ships. The relief dates to the eighth century BCE.

the Phoenicians guarded the secrets of their routes carefully, so no one else would be able to profit by them.

The Phoenicians' reputation as daring seafarers ensured that they were often hired by other nations to carry out adventurous voyages. Around 600 BCE, the Egyptian pharaoh Necho commissioned a Phoenician expedition to explore the coast of Africa. The ships sailed out through the Red Sea and returned to the Mediterranean several years later through the Strait of Gibraltar. In the fifth century BCE, the Greek historian Herodotus wrote the following account of the expedition: "They sailed south along the coast. In winter, the fleet looked for a safe haven where they sowed grain. After the harvest, the Phoenician ships moved on with fresh provisions on board. This way, the voyage around Africa took three years."

When they returned home, the Phoenician sailors claimed that they had seen the sun to the north. While this was unbelievable to their contemporaries, the report lends credence to the story that the Phoenicians passed the equator. In the Northern Hemisphere, the midday sun appears to be slightly to the south, because Earth is tilted on its axis. The reverse is true in the Southern Hemisphere—the sun appears to be to the north at midday. So, it seems likely that the Phoenicians did indeed sail completely around Africa.

The voyage of Hanno

One of the most famous Phoenician voyages took place in the late fifth century BCE, when a large expedition set out from Carthage with the explorer Hanno at its head. The purpose of the expedition was to found colonies along

PURPLE CLOTH

The Phoenicians were famous for their purple cloth, which came mainly from the city of Tyre. The color of the cloth was produced with the help of a purple dye obtained from the murex snail, a type of sea snail. These molluscs abounded in the sea around Tyre, and they were harvested by the thousands to make the dye. The process began when the shells were cracked open to remove the sea creature from inside. The soft bodies were then left to rot, producing a hideous stench for which Tyre was notorious. Once they had rotted, the bodies were pressed to extract a yellow liquid. When this liquid was boiled, it turned a dark purple.

Because only a tiny drop of liquid was yielded by each snail, an enormous number of molluscs were needed to produce a reasonable amount of the dye, making it a very expensive product. The Phoenician cloth dyers were skilled in using the liquid to dye cloth in colors varying from pale pink to dark purple. The purple cloth was much in demand because it was the color from which royal robes were made.

the Atlantic coast of Morocco. Hanno was provided with an enormous fleet and a vast number of colonists to carry out this task (see box, page 99).

The log of Hanno's voyage is unusual in that it has survived. The fact that so few Phoenician logs have come to light may be because they were kept secret and few copies or translations were ever made. The Phoenicians were anxious to guard their navigational secrets because those secrets were the basis of Phoenician prosperity. The Phoenicians maintained their secrets about trade in the Atlantic so successfully that the Greeks and Romans never discovered who the trading partners were.

One story that has survived relates how a Phoenician ship in the Atlantic deliberately changed course and ran aground when it realized that a Roman ship was spying on it. The Roman vessel followed its target onto the rocks and was wrecked as well. All hands were lost— only the Phoenician captain survived. When the captain finally returned home, he was rewarded with a large sum of money for eluding the attentions of the Romans and received full compensation for his lost cargo.

Despite the fact that the Phoenicians guarded their navigational secrets zealously, some of their knowledge did become known to the Greeks. Greek sailors from the island of Rhodes compiled a navigational manual called *The Captain of the Mediterranean*, which contained everything they knew about trade routes, winds, and ocean currents. It described the most favorable times for crossing the sea and gave advice on avoiding bad weather, rounding the ocean capes, and benefiting from the wind. This manual compiled by the Greeks remained until the 19th century CE an indispensable guide for vessels navigating the Mediterranean.

Methods of trade

The Phoenicians developed their own ingenious methods for trading with the indigenous peoples they encountered on their voyages to the Atlantic seaboard of Africa. According to Herodotus, the Carthaginians would sail to the west coast of Africa each year at the same time. They would deposit the goods they wanted to trade on a beach and then return to their ships. The local inhabitants would emerge from the jungle and place as much gold next to the merchandise as they saw fit. The Phoenicians would then return and inspect the gold, to determine whether the amount was sufficient. If it was not, they would return to their ships without touching anything. The Africans would then add more gold to the pile. This procedure might be repeated several times before the parties came to an agreement. Only when the

Phoenicians deemed the pile of gold to be sufficient would they take it and embark, leaving the local inhabitants to take the goods.

The alphabet

Despite their great exploits as seafarers, the most important legacy that the Phoenicians left is their alphabet. The earliest writing systems consisted of pictographs (hieroglyphs), simple pictures that represented objects or ideas. The beginning of a true alphabet occurs when a pictograph comes to represent part of the sound of a word, rather than the idea behind it.

The Phoenician settlements on the eastern shore of the Mediterranean were surrounded by four major cultures, each of which had its own script. To the north were the Hittites, who used a hieroglyphic script of such complexity that it

The remains of the forum at Carthage. Founded by exiles from Tyre, Carthage rose to become one of the western Mediterranean's most powerful city-states.

has still not been completely deciphered. To the east, the Mesopotamians had a cuneiform script that used symbols for the different syllables of a word. The Cretans and Mycenaeans to the west had two systems of writing (called Linear A and Linear B), as well as symbols to represent syllables. To the south, the Egyptians originally used hieroglyphs, but in the second millennium BCE, a script called the sacerdotal was developed. This script drew the hieroglyphs in an abbreviated form, in much the same way that a modern stenographer writes the alphabet in short form. The sacerdotal script bore some similarity to an alphabetical script but contained as many symbols as the hieroglyphic script. All of these writing systems used hundreds of different symbols and could not be called an alphabet in the modern sense of the word.

The first true alphabet, called North Semitic, originated on the eastern Mediterranean shore between 1700 and 1500 BCE and consisted of signs representing consonants, as do today's related Hebrew and Arabic variants. Other branches, including the Phoenician, developed from the original Semitic alphabet in the 11th century BCE.

The Phoenician script came to light in 1876, when a Syrian farmer turned up copper beakers bearing inscriptions from the time of King Hiram of Tyre, who ruled around 950 BCE. The farmer broke the beakers to sell the metal, and only a few fragments with inscriptions were recovered. The writing on those fragments is the known Semitic script and reads from right to left.

More finds were made in 1922, when a number of royal tombs were excavated

This colonnade is found in Tyre, which was one of the richest and most powerful of the Phoenician city-states. It was located in present-day Lebanon.

HANNO'S VOYAGE

The expedition of the Carthaginian explorer Hanno is well documented in the voyage's log, which has been preserved. The log records that Hanno "departed with 60 ships, each with 50 rowers. On board were men, women, and children, totalling 30,000."

Two days after sailing past the Strait of Gibraltar, the expedition made landfall and founded a city called Thymiaterion. "From there to Cape Libya," continues the log, "stretched a vast, tree-covered plain. There we built a temple for Poseidon, the god of the sea, and then sailed on to the south. We reached a lake where there were elephants and other wild animals. After another day of travel we founded new colonies and reached the river Lixos. A tribe of Berber shepherds lived on the banks of this river with their flocks; we befriended them and rested for a few days." They then sailed on for three more days, reaching a bay where they founded another colony. They believed this place to be as far to the west of the Strait of Gibraltar as Carthage was to the east. Eventually, the expedition reached a large river up which they sailed, coming to a lake on the banks of which rose great mountains. "On their slopes," records the log, "roamed wild people dressed in animal skins who pelted us with stones. From there we came to another wide river with many crocodiles and hippopotamuses." Back at the coast, they continued to sail south, noting that the land was inhabited by "Ethiopians" (by which they meant black Africans). After three weeks' sailing, they came to a gulf where many "wild people" lived. "Their bodies were completely covered with hair," notes the log, "and our interpreters called them gorillas. We tried to catch one but we did not succeed in catching a male because they climbed into trees and defended themselves with stones. We did catch three females, but because they bit everyone, we had to kill them. After we had skinned them, we took their hides back to the city of Carthage."

Although these hairy "people" were described as gorillas, it seems probable that they were actually chimpanzees, since gorillas would not have been so easy to catch. After this encounter, Hanno decided that the expedition was running out of provisions, and they turned back. It is not known quite how far south Hanno sailed, but it seems probable that the expedition traveled as far as Sierra Leone.

This stone relief depicts a Phoenician merchant vessel. The Phoenicians' considerable seafaring skills enabled them to make great voyages of discovery, such as that made by the explorer Hanno.

RELIGION AND SACRIFICE

The Phoenicians worshipped a large number of gods and goddesses, and each of the city-states had its own patron deity. For example, the citizens of Tyre worshipped a god called Melqart, who was a sun god. As might be expected from a god worshipped by seafarers, Melqart was also seen as a protector of navigators. When traders from Tyre set up a new colony, they made sacrifices to Melqart and would wait for a positive sign from the god before they settled. One of the first buildings to be constructed would be a temple to the god.

Melqart's consort was the fertility goddess Astarte, who was known by various names throughout the Mediterranean, including Astoret, Asherah, and Ashratu. She was closely linked to the Babylonian goddess Ishtar and the Egyptian goddess Isis. Astarte's equivalent in Carthage was Tanit. Although Tanit was the wife of the god Baal Hammon, she seems to have been seen as the more important deity. Like Astarte, Tanit was a fertility goddess.

Some historians believe that the Phoenicians practiced some form of child sacrifice. According to Greek writers such as Diodorus Siculus (first century BCE), children would be burned in sacred fires in front of their parents. Diodorus wrote that hundreds of children were sacrificed in Carthage when the city was besieged by Greek Sicilian forces in 310 BCE. Other historians dispute the view. They argue that the burnt remains of children's bones found in sacred hearths came from children who had died naturally and point out that most of the stories of child sacrifice come from cultures that were enemies of the Phoenicians.

This gold necklace was made by Phoenician craftsmen around the fifth century BCE.

The ruins of the Hall of the Ambassador at Ugarit. Ugarit was one of the wealthiest Phoenician cities.

in Byblos. The stone coffin of King Ahiram, who ruled in the early 10th century BCE, contained an elaborate text in the linear Phoenician alphabet.

The Greeks adopted the Phoenician alphabet in the eighth century BCE, making only minor changes to the shape of the letters. The Greeks expanded the 22 Phoenician consonants to 24 and made some symbols serve as vowels. After around 500 BCE, the Greeks started writing from left to right.

The Greek alphabet was adopted and adapted throughout the Mediterranean world. When it passed to the Romans, they spread it via Latin throughout the Roman Empire. The Greek alphabet was therefore destined to become the basis of all Western alphabets.

Foreign domination again

In 842 BCE, most of the Phoenician cities on the eastern Mediterranean coast lost their independence when they became absorbed into the Assyrian Empire during the campaigns of conquest of the Assyrian king Shalmaneser III. From this point onward, the Phoenicians came under the control of a succession of foreign powers.

Phoenicia remained part of the Assyrian Empire until the late seventh century BCE and then came under the control of the Babylonians. The region fell to the Persian forces of Cyrus the Great in 539 BCE. Under Persian rule, the cities enjoyed some freedoms and were able to prosper again commercially, but Phoenicia was not to survive. In 330 BCE, the region was conquered by the Macedonian general Alexander the Great. Finally, in 64 BCE, Phoenicia became part of the Roman Empire and lost all separate identity.

See also:

The Assyrians (page 102) • The Israelites (page 116)

THE ASSYRIANS

Known for their ruthlessness in subjugating their enemies, the Assyrians dominated large sections of western Asia for much of the second and first millenniums BCE. A visual record of their conquests can be found at their ancient capital of Nimrud.

Assyria was one of the earliest empires to be established in western Asia. The core of the Assyrian heartland lay to the north of Babylonia, between the Tigris River to the west and the Zagros Mountains to the east. The discovery of two Neanderthal skulls in the area showed that the area has been inhabited since Paleolithic times. There is also evidence that early farmers settled in this fertile area around the ninth millennium BCE. They grew wheat and barley, kept domesticated animals, and built houses of clay. They are also known to have baked bread in clay ovens, spun thread using hand spindles, woven cloth, and made tools, ornaments, and seals out of stone.

During the third millennium BCE, the region came under the influence of the Akkadian civilization, and the inhabitants adopted the Akkadian language and cuneiform script. When the southern empires of Sumer and Akkad collapsed around 2000 BCE, a distinct Assyrian culture began to emerge. However, nothing was known of this culture until the 19th century CE, when two outstanding archaeologists—Paul Emile Botta and Austen Henry Layard—excavated the cities of Nineveh, Nimrud, and Dur Sharrukin (Khorsabad). The spectacular finds that Botta and Layard made unravelled the story of one of the great lost civilizations of western Asia.

Historians usually divide the history of the Assyrian Empire into three periods: the Old Empire (c. 2000–1760 BCE), the Middle Empire (c. 1363–1000 BCE), and the New Empire (c. 1000–612 BCE). During the period of the Old Empire, the Assyrians established a number of city-states, including Ashur, Nineveh, and Arbela. Each city consisted of a palace, temples, and a maze of houses, all enclosed within a city wall. Ashur, named after the god of the same name, was the center of a remarkable trading network. A merchant colony was set up in the city of Kanesh in Anatolia, and pottery vessels full of cuneiform texts discovered there give a picture of a flourishing trade in copper and textiles, carried by caravans of donkeys. This lucrative enterprise was controlled by just 10 or 15 Assyrian families, and their burial sites discovered in Ashur attest to their great wealth.

The rule of Shamshi-Adad I

From around 1813 BCE, Assyria came under the rule of Shamshi-Adad I (ruled c. 1813–1781 BCE), a prince of an Amorite dynasty. He had imperialist

These remains of a ziggurat are located at Nimrud. The city reached the height of its wealth in the ninth century BCE, hundreds of years after it was founded.

102

ambitions and conquered an area that extended from Assyria in the east to Mari on the Euphrates River in the west and Babylonia in the south. Ruling from Ashur, Shamshi-Adad established what was probably the first centrally organized empire of the ancient Middle East. At the death of Shamshi-Adad, his son Ishme-Dagan I succeeded to the throne. During Ishme-Dagan's reign, King Hammurabi of Babylonia captured Ashur, bringing the Assyrian Old Empire to an end. Assyria became part of the Babylonian Empire around 1760 BCE.

Toward the end of the third millennium BCE, a new population group arrived in Mesopotamia. The Hurrians founded large colonies on the upper reaches of the Euphrates and Tigris rivers. These colonies were the forerunners of the Mitanni Empire. By around 1500 BCE, the Hurrian Mitanni kingdom had come to dominate northern Mesopotamia. The kingdom subjugated Assyria, maintaining regional control for the next century, while the Hittites were establishing their rival empire to the north. Around 1363 BCE, while the Mitanni were preoccupied with the Hittites, the Assyrian king Ashur-uballit I successfully attacked the Mitanni and won back Assyrian freedom. This marked the beginning of the Middle Empire.

The Middle Empire

As head of the newly independent Assyria, Ashur-uballit called himself the "Great King" and considered himself the equal of the king of Egypt. Ashur-uballit named Assyria the "Land of Ashur," and he and his successors set about restoring the might of the empire.

After Ashur-uballit's death in 1328 BCE, a drawn-out war with Babylonia ensued. Successive Assyrian kings also led campaigns to the east and north to suppress hostile tribes that threatened the borders. To the west, the Assyrian army reached the Euphrates River around 1300 BCE, under the leadership of Adad-nirari I (ruled c. 1305–1274 BCE). In 1250 BCE, Adad-nirari's son King Shalmaneser I succeeded in annexing the Mitanni Empire, thereby greatly extending his own empire.

Shalmaneser's son Tukulti-Ninurta I (ruled c. 1233–1197 BCE) was a gifted sovereign under whom Assyria achieved unprecedented power. He took on the might of Babylonia, defeated its army, sacked the city of Babylon, and plundered its temples. He was the first king to carry out large-scale deportations to ensure peace in the empire, but his ruthless methods made him so unpopular that eventually his sons instigated a rebellion in which he was killed.

The coming of the Sea Peoples

Around 1200 BCE, a period of great unrest began in the Mesopotamian region. A group of invaders known to the Egyptians as the Sea Peoples defeated the Hittites in Anatolia, while the Aramaeans made incursions into Mesopotamia. The Assyrian king Tiglath-pileser I (ruled c. 1114–1076 BCE) reacted strongly to this threat, raiding and razing Aramaean villages and seizing or massacring anyone who did not flee. Nevertheless, the Aramaeans continued their onslaughts. By around 1000 BCE, they were firmly entrenched in the west and seemed poised to take over the entire Assyrian kingdom. Assyria, and indeed the whole region, was entering a dark age, perhaps caused, and certainly made worse, by drought and famine.

During the Middle Empire period, the Assyrian state had developed into a strong military power. Constant battles to protect the Assyrian borders had honed an efficient army (see box, page 108), which was greatly strengthened by the introduction of the horse-drawn chariot. The wealth of the state depended on

THE GROWTH OF THE ASSYRIAN EMPIRE

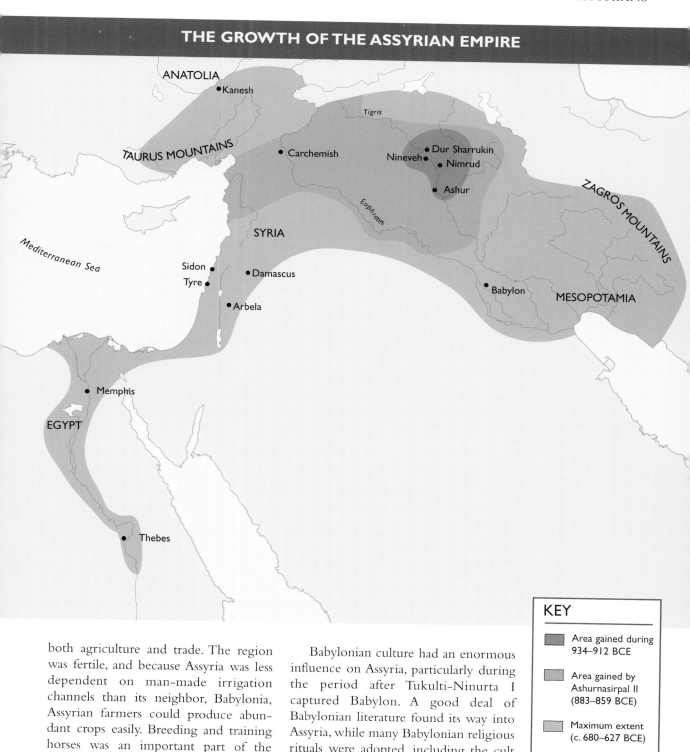

ANATOLIA

• Kanesh

TAURUS MOUNTAINS

Tigris

• Carchemish

Nineveh • • Dur Sharrukin
• Nimrud

Ashur

ZAGROS MOUNTAINS

Euphrates

SYRIA

Mediterranean Sea

Sidon •
Tyre •

• Damascus

• Arbela

• Babylon

MESOPOTAMIA

• Memphis

EGYPT

• Thebes

KEY

Area gained during
934–912 BCE

Area gained by
Ashurnasirpal II
(883–859 BCE)

Maximum extent
(c. 680–627 BCE)

both agriculture and trade. The region was fertile, and because Assyria was less dependent on man-made irrigation channels than its neighbor, Babylonia, Assyrian farmers could produce abundant crops easily. Breeding and training horses was an important part of the economy, and Assyrian horses were famous throughout the Middle East.

Babylonian culture had an enormous influence on Assyria, particularly during the period after Tukulti-Ninurta I captured Babylon. A good deal of Babylonian literature found its way into Assyria, while many Babylonian religious rituals were adopted, including the cult of the god Marduk. The Assyrians took over the Babylonian calendar and

Assyrian soldiers are depicted defending a fortress in this relief from the eighth century BCE.

changed their system of weights and measures to that of the Babylonians. The Babylonian influence can also be seen in Assyrian art and architecture.

Many of the tablets discovered by archaeologists have provided a comprehensive picture of the legal system that was in place in the Middle Empire. Punishments for infractions of the law were extremely severe, ranging from beatings to mutilation and death. Women had very few rights. A husband could divorce his wife at will, and if she committed adultery, he could maim her or even kill her. Women led very restricted lives and had to wear veils whenever they went out in public.

The New Empire

By around 900 BCE, the Hittite Empire had disappeared. Mesopotamia and Syria were suffering under attacks from the Aramaean tribes, whose centers of power included southern Babylonia and the area surrounding Damascus. Assyria, which was increasingly on the defensive, had been forced back from the border formed by the Euphrates River in the west.

Around the beginning of the ninth century BCE, things began to change. Two kings—Adad-nirari II (ruled c. 911–891 BCE) and Tukulti-Ninurta II (ruled c. 890–884 BCE)—succeeded in winning back territory from the Aramaeans and regaining the banks of the Euphrates River. Their successes marked a turning point in Assyrian fortunes. Ashurnasirpal II, the son of Tukulti-Ninurta II, ruled from 883 to 859 BCE and continued his father's policy of reconquest, isolating the Aramaean city-states one by one and destroying them. He was a brilliant and ruthless general, and his own accounts of his campaigns testify to their terrifying cruelty. It was his custom to impale his defeated enemies on stakes, flay them alive, or behead them. He also deported the local citizenry en masse, thereby robbing the conquered region of its indigenous people and creating a subjugated population throughout the empire.

Military tactics

Ashurnasirpal's campaigns were helped by the fact that he made substantial use of units of cavalry, in addition to his war chariots and infantry. He also used mobile battering rams to break down the walls of cities under siege. Once he had taken a city, he made sure that Assyrian officials quickly took over its administration, thereby ensuring that the new conquest was incorporated into the Assyrian Empire smoothly and efficiently without any loss of time.

By attacking the regions on Assyria's immediate borders, Ashurnasirpal was able to extend his rule as far as the Mediterranean Sea. He annexed Phoenician coastal cities and small states on the Mediterranean coast and forced them to pay annual tribute to Assyria. It was not advisable to resist the Assyrian army; no one was spared if a city had to be taken by force.

The following is Ashurnasirpal's own account of the taking of the fortress of Hulai: "I surrounded the city with the main force of my troops. After a wild battle in the field, I took it. I slew 600 of his warriors with my weapons; 3,000 prisoners I burned in a great fire; I did not take a single hostage.... I stacked the bodies like towers; the young men and girls I burned alive. I skinned the king of Hulai alive and hung his skin on the city walls. I demolished and burned the city."

LAYARD'S DISCOVERIES

Much of the existing knowledge about the Assyrians is the result of the work of British archaeologist Austen Henry Layard (1817–1894). Layard began excavating the ancient Assyrian city of Nimrud in 1845. At the time, he was unaware that he had uncovered the palace and capital of Ashurnasirpal II. However, as Layard and his team worked on, they discovered a number of magnificent artifacts that revealed much about the life of the Assyrian king who ruled in the ninth century BCE.

Among the treasures found at Nimrud was a statue of Ashurnasirpal himself, which had once stood in the temple of the goddess Ishtar. There were a number of huge stone sphinxes, which had guarded the palace. There were also relief sculptures depicting scenes from royal life. One object that contained a number of such reliefs was the Black Obelisk, a stele that stood nearly 7 feet (2.1 m) tall. The stele, which was crowned by three steps in the shape of a ziggurat, showed scenes of foreign kings paying tribute to Shalmaneser III, Ashurnasirpal's son and successor. Assyrian kings often collected animals as trophies, and the illustrations on the obelisk show a number of exotic beasts, including an elephant and a rhinoceros, being brought to the king.

Cultural impact

Despite the many atrocities that he committed, Ashurnasirpal proved to be a positive cultural force. He commissioned architects, sculptors, and artists to build or enlarge several temples and palaces, and the resulting works exhibited a quality never before achieved. He restored the city of Nimrud (ancient Calah), making it his capital in place of Ashur. This was a mammoth project. The city wall itself needed around 70 million bricks of sun-dried clay to enclose an area of around 864 acres (350 ha). Inside this wall was built a magnificent palace, which covered an area of 269,000 square feet (25,000 m²).

The palace, based on a modified version of an ancient pattern, had two com-

THE ASSYRIAN ARMY

During the New Empire, the Assyrian army developed from a part-time amateur force that was conscripted for plundering raids to a highly professional standing army that was one of the most efficient and deadly fighting forces ever known. Up until the ninth century BCE, the army consisted mainly of peasants and farmers who were forced to join the king on his annual campaigns. In theory, all men had to do military duty, but many wealthy Assyrians managed to evade service by providing slaves instead. These conscripts, led by a core of professional soldiers, consisted mostly of light infantrymen armed with bows and arrows, slings, pikes, spears, battle-axes, and swords. Of these light infantrymen, the archers were the most important. Troops in the heavy infantry were also equipped with armor.

By the ninth century BCE, a standing army had been formed. The commander in chief was the king, who often led campaigns in person. The bulk of the army consisted of foreign contingents of foot soldiers conscripted from various subjugated lands and led by Assyrian officers. The army was divided into units of varying size. The company, which was the basic unit, consisted of 50 men under the command of a captain.

The elite of the army were the charioteers. Each chariot carried a driver, an archer, and usually one or two shield bearers to protect the driver and archer. The chariots were backed up by cavalry, which rode bareback and operated in pairs. One cavalryman wielded a short bow, while his partner carried a shield to protect him.

The marching army was followed by engineers who would build bridges and other structures. Engineers were also in charge of battering rams, siege towers, and other devices, such as scaling ladders, that were used in siege warfare. The battering rams were contained in wheeled huts that both protected the ram itself and carried archers who could shoot at attackers.

The preferred tactic in conquering a new region was to choose one particular city and lay siege to it. Once a breach in the city's walls was made, the army poured through and proceeded to massacre both the defenders and the citizens. The mutilated bodies would then be hung on the city's walls as a warning to others.

A battering ram is shown breaking down the walls of a city in this bronze relief from the ninth century BCE.

plexes of halls built around two central courtyards and connected by a narrow throne room measuring 65 by 33 feet (20 by 10 m). This double architectural design may reflect Aramaean influence.

Art of intimidation

The state rooms and living quarters of the palace at Nimrud were decorated with murals carved out of limestone blocks, each measuring around 6.5 feet (2 m) high and 13 feet (4 m) wide. Many of these murals showed mythological scenes, but there were also scenes of war, which were intended to intimidate those who saw them. In the throne room, there was a continuous pageant of images, in which the king was the main character. The king was shown as the upholder and protector of fertility, a typical motif in Mesopotamia and, indeed, the entire ancient world.

These royal reliefs are unique in terms of their style and content. For the first time, each image portrays a historical event. Many of these wall reliefs were painted in bright colors, representing the absolute height of Mesopotamian art. Above the friezes were more highly colored murals painted directly on to the plaster of the walls. The calibre of the work is all the more remarkable because most of the craftsmen working on the palace were prisoners of war or forced labor conscripted from the far-flung reaches of the empire.

The entrances to the halls and courtyards were guarded by massive three-dimensional sculptures of bull figures with wings and human heads. These figures had the purpose both of protecting the palace against evil spirits and of warning those who came within the palace precincts that the power of the Assyrian king reached far and wide.

In 879 BCE, Ashurnasirpal celebrated the completion of his royal palace by giving an enormous banquet, to which

he invited almost 70,000 guests. The festivities lasted for ten days, during which time 14,000 sheep were consumed and 10,000 vessels of wine were drunk.

A warlike king

Ashurnasirpal's son, Shalmaneser III (ruled c. 858–824 BCE), was as ruthless as Ashurnasirpal and continued his expansionist policies. Shalmaneser crossed the Euphrates 25 times to do battle against the Aramaeans, conducting 32 campaigns in 35 years. However, not all his campaigns were successful. Although Shalmaneser managed to conquer northern Syria, he was unable to subdue

This relief shows an angel or spirit, one of many mythological beings depicted in Assyrian art.

109

Damascus, even though his army besieged the city in 841 BCE. Shalmaneser also campaigned against a new kingdom in the north, Urartu, which was threatening Assyria.

Shalmaneser completed the construction of Nimrud begun by his father and built many other temples and palaces throughout the empire. He commissioned sculptors and artists to produce statues and stelae, including the famous Black Obelisk (see box, page 107), which shows the kings of Israel paying tribute to Assyria. The reliefs in hammered bronze, called the Bronze Gates of Balawat, which once decorated the temple doors in the town of Balawat, northeast of Nimrud, depicted Shalmaneser's victories over the Phoenicians as well as other subjugated territories. The bronze reliefs also showed the rulers of both Tyre and Sidon bringing tribute.

Under Shalmaneser's immediate successors, Assyria entered a period of decline. There was increasing civil unrest, and in the provinces, some of the nobles who held vast territories acted as if they were independent rulers. Over the generations, thousands of Aramaeans who had been transported to Assyria to work on building projects had been assimilated into Assyrian society, and many of them rose to high positions in the civil service. As a result, the Assyrian language was gradually replaced by Aramaic in common usage.

This bronze bowl, made in the eighth century BCE, is believed to be of Phoenician origin, even though it was found at Nimrud. Archaeologists believe that the bowl was brought back to Assyria as war booty.

Coup d'état

In the middle of the eighth century BCE, a military coup brought a new king to the throne. Tiglath-pileser III (ruled c. 746–727 BCE) embarked energetically on restoring and expanding the empire. To this end, he created a regular standing army. Instead of conscripting farmers each year for a campaign, he formed an army of professionals, consisting largely of foreign contingents, with chariots and cavalry as its core. To break the power of the provincial governors, he reduced the size of the provinces. He also abolished tax exemptions for temples and major cities so taxation would be spread more evenly.

After he had restored civil order at home, Tiglath-pileser embarked on a campaign to drive the Urartians out of Syria. Once he had defeated the Urartian army in battle, he besieged the Syrian capital of Arpad, which had become an ally of Urartu. After three years, he took the city. In true Assyrian style, he put all the inhabitants to the sword and razed the city itself to the ground. Then, instead of appointing a local king as his vassal, Tiglath-pileser appointed an Assyrian governor. He then invaded Israel, annexing large territories there, and took Damascus in 732 BCE. By his campaigns, he extended the empire to the Taurus Mountains in the north and the Sinai Desert in the south.

Tiglath-pileser quickly turned his attention to Babylonia. Following the death of the king Nabu-nasir, the Babylonian throne had been claimed by an Aramaean. Tiglath-pileser drove out the Aramaeans and had himself crowned king of Babylon—under the name of Pulu—in 729 BCE. This action united Assyria and Babylonia under one rule.

In the subsequent years, Tiglath-pileser devoted himself to rebuilding and improving Nimrud and its palace. He commissioned new reliefs, many of them showing gruesome scenes of battles and executions, for the palace walls. After his death, he was succeeded by his son Shalmaneser V (ruled c. 727–722 BCE), who spent three years vainly besieging Samaria, the capital of Israel. He proved to be more successful in conquering the rest of the country, but a revolt in Ashur put an end to the reign of Shalmaneser.

Sargon II

The next great ruler of Assyria was Sargon II, who ruled between 722 and 705 BCE. It is not clear exactly who Sargon was, but he may have been a younger brother of Shalmaneser V. In taking the name Sargon, which means "legitimate king," he may have been trying to bolster a weak claim to the throne. To curry favor with the priests and merchants, the first thing he did at the beginning of his reign was to restore some of the privileges they had lost under Tiglath-pileser, particularly the tax exemptions

The Black Obelisk of Shalmaneser III, made in the ninth century BCE, is decorated with scenes of the king receiving tribute.

previously enjoyed by the temples and major cities.

Sargon continued the empire building of his predecessor and added further territories. He subjugated Urartu once again and took Carchemish. In 712 BCE, he defeated a coalition of the Syrian and Phoenician cities, annexing numerous states in Syria and southern Anatolia. He campaigned against the Medes on the eastern border and defeated the Aramaeans in the central Tigris Valley and the Chaldeans in the lower Euphrates Valley. In the subjugated regions, Sargon built mighty fortresses.

At the time of Sargon's accession, the throne of Babylonia had been seized by a Chaldean, Merodach-baladan II. Not until 710 BCE did Sargon find the time to move on the usurper, who fled. Merodach-baladan had been so unpopular with the Babylonians that they welcomed Sargon with relief, and he became the first Assyrian to be crowned king of Babylon under his own name.

By this time, Sargon's vast empire extended from the border of Egypt in the southwest to the Zagros Mountains in the east and from the Taurus Mountains in the northwest to the Persian Gulf in the southeast. Sargon divided this empire into some 70 provinces, each headed by a governor who was directly responsible to the king. In his capital of Nimrud, Sargon created a central administrative organization and delegated some of his own power to his son Sennacherib.

Toward the end of his reign, Sargon started on the

construction of a new capital, the famous city of Khorsabad, 8 miles (12.9 km) north of Nineveh. This city was originally called Dur Sharrukin (meaning "Sargon's Fortress"), and it was intended to be more elegant and refined than earlier Assyrian building complexes. However, following Sargon's death in 705 BCE, work on the new capital ceased, and when archaeologists first discovered the site in 1840 CE, the city was just as it had been when it was abandoned 2,500 years earlier.

Under Sargon II, Assyria had reached the peak of its power. However, in 705 BCE, during a minor campaign in western Iran, Sargon was ambushed and slain. His body was left unburied to be eaten by vultures. This inglorious death made a great impression on the world, and his son Sennacherib (ruled 704–681 BCE)

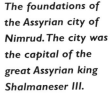

The foundations of the Assyrian city of Nimrud. The city was the capital of the great Assyrian king Shalmaneser III.

ordered his priests to find out what his father had done to incur the wrath of the gods. The priests' answer was that the gods had been offended by the construction of the new capital.

Trouble in Babylon

Before Sargon's death, Sennacherib had quarreled with his father, and on ascending the throne, he seemed determined to turn his back on his late father's memory. He abandoned the half-built city of Dur Sharrukin and, after residing in Ashur for a few years, made Nineveh his capital. In all the many inscriptions of Sennacherib's reign, there is no mention of Sargon.

Soon after Sennacherib's accession, there was trouble with Babylon. In 703 BCE, Merodach-baladan attempted to seize the throne again, allying himself

with the city of Elam, Assyria's age-old enemy. After a nine-month campaign, Sennacherib finally succeeded in defeating this coalition, although Merodach-baladan escaped. In order to reassert control, Sennacherib deported more than 200,000 people from southern Mesopotamia and put an Assyrian puppet king on the Babylonian throne.

Turning his attention to the west, Sennacherib then marched into Syria and Palestine and laid siege to Jerusalem. He was hoping to clear the way for his armies to march on Egypt, but Jerusalem would not yield. Eventually, with his army decimated by sickness, Sennacherib was forced to withdraw.

Meanwhile, in Babylon, Merodach-baladan was stirring up a renewed rebellion. Assyria's puppet king allied himself with Merodach-baladan, but Sennacherib lost no time in crushing the revolt and putting his own son on the Babylonian throne. The Elamites continued to foment Babylonian rebellions, and when the Babylonians handed over Sennacherib's

This ancient relief, discovered during excavations of Nineveh, depicts two Assyrian warriors hunting a lion.

A QUEEN'S CURSE

While most of the great archaeological discoveries relating to the Assyrian Empire occurred in the 19th century CE, one happened a lot more recently—in 1989. Workers removing dirt from one of the palaces at Nimrud stumbled across an air vent to a hidden tomb. Further investigation by the Iraqi archaeologist Muzahim Mahmoud Hussein revealed the skeleton of Queen Yabahya, the wife of Tiglath-pileser III.

The skeleton had been buried with around 80 gold items, including personal jewelry, a golden bowl bearing the queen's name, and a number of rosettes that had been sprinkled over her body. However, the tomb also contained a less pleasant surprise—a curse. An inscription on a marble slab warned that anyone who disturbed the queen's resting place would suffer an eternity of sleeplessness.

son to the Elamites, Sennacherib acted decisively. In 689 BCE, he inflicted a crushing defeat on both states. He then destroyed the city of Babylon. After plundering and leveling the temples, he had the Euphrates River diverted to flood the ruins. In a symbolic act, statues of the gods of the holy city were taken to Ashur as prisoners. This sacrilege offended even some Assyrians, who feared retribution from the Babylonian god Marduk for the deliberate violation of his temple.

Rebuilding Nineveh and Babylon

Sennacherib chose Nineveh to be his capital city. He carried out extensive renovations there and built himself a magnificent palace with beautiful gardens. To bring water to these gardens, an immense aqueduct was constructed, using around two million limestone blocks. The palace itself was decorated with many reliefs, some of which showed enormous statues of bulls being transported over land and water. Other scenes showed military life, battles, and the mass deportations of conquered peoples. To make the palace of Sennacherib as splendid as possible, Assyrian artists were given a free rein in its design.

In 681 BCE, Sennacherib was suddenly assassinated—widely seen as just retribution for his treatment of the god Marduk. Sennacherib was succeeded by his son Esarhaddon (ruled 680–669 BCE).

Esarhaddon was not the eldest son, and it is thought that he owed his throne to the influence of his mother, Naqia. She was a princess from western Syria and, for a long time, controlled state affairs from behind the scenes. To appease Marduk, Esarhaddon set about recon-

structing Babylon, in particular the temples of Marduk. In the west, Esarhaddon attacked Egypt, capturing Memphis in 671 BCE. This victory was the major military achievement of his reign; he died during a second expedition to Egypt in 669 BCE.

The last great king

Once again, Naqia arranged the succession, placing her youngest grandson, Ashurbanipal (ruled c. 668–627 BCE), on the throne and appointing one of his older brothers viceroy of Babylon. Ashurbanipal continued his father's Egyptian campaign, putting down revolts and conquering as far south as Thebes. However, later in Ashurbanipal's reign, the Egyptians succeeded in regaining their independence and driving out the Assyrian garrisons.

In southern Babylonia, the Elamites continued their attacks. Ashurbanipal dispatched an army to defeat them, but his brother, the Babylonian viceroy, rebelled and a protracted war ensued.

Located on the banks of the Tigris, the city of Nineveh was perfectly situated as a trading center.

This relief sculpture depicts the Assyrian king Ashurbanipal riding in a chariot. Ashurbanipal was one of the last kings of the Assyrian Empire.

The Assyrians laid siege to Babylon for three years. The city was taken in 648 BCE, and the palace was burned to the ground with the viceroy inside.

Determined to subdue the Elamites once and for all, Ashurbanipal invaded their territory and attacked the capital, Susa. The city fell in 646 BCE, after which the Assyrians totally destroyed it and annexed the whole state. This victory was to be the Assyrians' last great military success; thereafter, the empire went into rapid decline.

Ashurbanipal was a man of many talents. Besides being an able military commander and an enthusiastic hunter of big game, he was a mathematician and scientist and was able to read both Sumerian and Akkadian. At his palace at Nineveh, he founded a library in which several copies of the more important works were kept. The library consisted of approximately 25,000 clay tablets, which included new copies of a large number of old texts. This remarkable archive has been a valuable source of Assyrian history for archaeologists.

End of an empire

In the last years of Ashurbanipal's life, civil war broke out between his twin sons. The weakened empire was not able to withstand an onslaught from the Medes, who captured the city of Ashur in 614 BCE. With the help of the Babylonians, the Medes took Nineveh in 612 BCE and razed it to the ground. The Assyrian army, under the last Assyrian king, Ashur-uballit II (ruled 612–609 BCE), fled to Harran in the west. When the Assyrian army was finally defeated at Harran in 609 BCE, the defeat marked the end of the Assyrian Empire.

See also:

The Babylonians (page 62)

THE ISRAELITES

The Israelites were a Semitic people who lived in the eastern Mediterranean region. The stories contained in the Old Testament of the Bible are an important source of information about the Israelites' history.

The Israelites of the Bible were descended from pastoral nomads, originally from Arabia, who from around 3000 BCE onwards settled in Mesopotamia, along the eastern coast of the Mediterranean Sea, and in the delta of the Nile River. These nomads were Semites, speakers of Semitic languages, such as Hebrew and Arabic.

In southern Mesopotamia, Semitic nomads settled alongside the Sumerians and later established the Akkadian dynasty—founded by Sargon of Akkad around 2300 BCE. The Akkadians conquered a string of prominent city-states including Ur and Umma. In Syria, Semitic groups established powerful kingdoms at Ebla and Mari.

The land of Canaan

Another Semitic group settled along the eastern shores of the Mediterranean. The long strip of largely fertile land that stretched from southern Anatolia southward to the border with Egypt is known in the Bible as Canaan. Much of Old Testament history records strife between the Canaanites (the earliest Semitic inhabitants of Canaan) and later arrivals, who included the Israelites' ancestors, the Hebrews.

By the 12th century BCE, the Canaanites' kingdom was reduced to the narrow piece of coastal territory that makes up modern Lebanon. Around that time, the eastern Mediterranean coast and Egypt came under repeated attacks from armed raiders who were known to the Egyptians as the Sea Peoples—because they came by boat. Among the raiders were the Philistines, who may have come from Crete. The Philistines proved to be persistent enemies of the Israelites. In biblical accounts, the Philistines are presented as boorish and uncultured, although there is no historical evidence that they lacked artistic ability or interest. The Philistines gave their name to the much-contested land of Palestine.

From the 12th century BCE to the ninth century BCE, the Phoenicians, descendants of earlier Semitic occupants of Canaan, rose to prominence in this coastal area of Canaan. They established a wide commercial empire, with trading posts as far afield as Spain and northern Africa. They were brilliant navigators and expert boatbuilders. In 814 BCE, they founded the great ancient city of Carthage in northern Africa. The city became one of the most important trading powers of the Mediterranean region.

This mosaic from the Basilica of San Marco in Venice depicts the head of Solomon, king of the Israelites. He is most famous for building the temple in Jerusalem. The mosaic was created in the 14th century CE.

THE KINGDOM OF DAVID AND SOLOMON

CYPRUS

Byblos

SYRIA

Sidon

CANAAN

Tyre

Damascus

Mediterranean Sea

Samaria • Shechem

ISRAEL

Ashdod Ekron
Ashkelon • Jerusalem
Gath

Gaza • Hebron

EGYPT

KEY

Area under
direct rule
(c. 1000–928 BCE)

Vassal states
(c. 1000–928 BCE)

Canaanite enclaves
conquered by
David

Area ceded to
Tyre by Solomon

The origins of the Israelites

Out of the many Semitic nomads, one group—the Hebrews—later came to be known as the Israelites. According to the Bible, both Semites and Hebrews were named after ancestors—the Semites because they could all trace their ancestry back to Shem, eldest son of Noah, who built the Ark and survived the Great Flood; the Hebrews because they were all descended from Heber, one of Shem's great-grandsons.

The earliest historical reference to the Hebrews (under the name Hapiru) is found in the so-called Mari tablets. Made around 1800 BCE, these clay records were found in the remains of the palace of King Zimrilim at Mari, a Mesopotamian city on the Euphrates River (now Tall al-Hariri in Syria). The earliest historical reference to Israel and the Israelites comes much later, around 1209 BCE, in the Merneptah stele—a carved stone column recording the achievements of an ancient Egyptian pharaoh, Merneptah, who ruled between 1213 and 1203 BCE. The stele gives an account of Merneptah's victory in battle over Libyan troops and the armies of the Sea Peoples, and it mentions his defeat in western Canaan of forces from Ashkelon, Gezer, Yanoam, and Israel. It declares: "Canaan is taken prisoner and in despair. Ashkelon is defeated, Gezer taken, Yanoam reduced to nothing; Israel also is brought to ruin, its people slain."

Almost all knowledge of the Israelites' earliest history and first migrations comes from the Book of Genesis— the first book of the Hebrew Bible and of the Old Testament in the Christian Bible. This biblical account identifies one man, Abraham (originally called Abram), as the ancestor from whom all the Israelites were descended and as the founder of their religion, Judaism.

Abram's journey to Canaan

According to the Bible, Abram lived in the city of Ur on the lower reaches of the Euphrates River in southern Mesopotamia, probably around 1800 BCE. Located on the same site as modern Tall al-Muqayyar, around 200 miles (300 km) southeast of Baghdad in Iraq, Ur was one of Sumer's major city-states, an important cultural and commercial center.

Abram, according to the account in Genesis, initially left Ur in the company of his wife Sarai (later called Sarah), his nephew Lot, and his father Terah and traveled as far as Harran, which was an ancient pilgrimage site for devotees of the Sumerian moon god Nanna and is now located in southeast Turkey. After staying at Haran for some time, and following the death of Terah, Abram was visited by God (the single god, Yahweh, later worshipped by the Israelites) and instructed to journey to a new land and found a great nation. Abram obeyed and

departed to Canaan. His party made its first encampment in Canaan at Shechem. Genesis adds: "And the Canaanites were then in the land."

God promised the land of Canaan to Abram's descendants, but Abram was childless; his wife Sarai was unable to bear children. Initially, Abram adopted a manservant, Eliezer, as his heir. Then, Sarai gave Abram her maidservant, a young Egyptian woman named Hagar. Abram and Hagar had a son, Ishmael. Subsequently, God declared his intention

The victory stele of Merneptah (an Egyptian pharaoh) contains the earliest recorded mention of the Israelites. It was made around 1209 BCE.

to make Abram the "father of many nations" and again agreed an "everlasting covenant" with him to give Abram and his descendants the land of Canaan. God declared that Abram should be known as Abraham and Sarai as Sarah and promised that Sarah would bear Abraham a son. It would be with this child that God would keep his covenant.

Sarah's son, Isaac, was the father of Jacob, who is celebrated in Judaism as the forefather of the Jews. Hagar's son, Ishmael, on the other hand, is celebrated in Islam as the forefather of the Arab peoples. Both Abraham (Ibrahim) and Ishmael are viewed as prophets.

The Sacrifice of Isaac, painted in 1604 CE by Caravaggio, depicts the moment when an angel sent by God prevents Abraham from sacrificing his son Isaac.

Israel's ties with Egypt

The biblical account of the history of the Israelites continues with a description of how Isaac's son Jacob tricked his twin brother Esau out of his birthright and fled to his uncle, Laban, back at Harran. Jacob married Laban's daughters, Leah and Rachel. They and their servants bore Jacob the 12 sons who traditionally established the twelve tribes of Israel. Jacob and his extended family subsequently left Harran and returned to Canaan. On the way, after a nocturnal encounter with an angel of God, Jacob received the new name of Israel. After some time in Canaan, Israel, probably

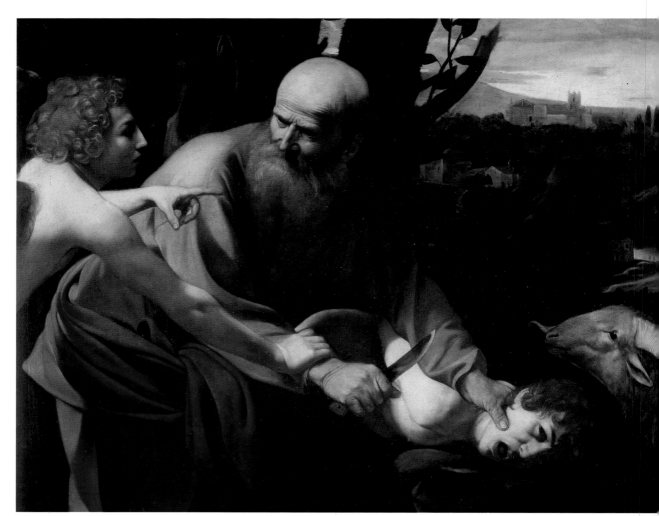

THE TRIBES OF ISRAEL

According to biblical accounts, Jacob (later known as Israel) had 13 children (12 boys and a girl) by his two wives, Leah and Rachel, and their two maidservants, Bilhah (Rachel's servant) and Zilpah (Leah's servant). Leah bore six sons, Reuben, Simeon, Levi, Judah, Issachar, and Zebulun, and a daughter, Dinah. Rachel's sons were Joseph and Benjamin. Bilhah's sons were Dan and Naphtali, while Zilpah's sons were Gad and Asher.

The descendants of the 12 sons of Jacob later formed the 12 Tribes of Israel. Following the Exodus from Egypt and the entry into the Promised Land, Joshua divided the land of Canaan among the tribes. However, the tribe of Levi did not receive any land because the members were hereditary priests. In listings that record land apportioned to the tribes, the tribe of Levi does not appear and the tribe of Joseph is replaced by two tribes, those of his sons Ephraim and Manasseh.

Subsequently, when Israel divided following the death of Solomon, the northern Kingdom of Israel, based on Shechem, was founded by the tribes of Reuben, Simeon, Levi, Issachar, Zebulun, Dan, Naphtali, Gad, Asher, and Ephraim and Manasseh, while the southern Kingdom of Judah was founded by the tribes of Judah and Benjamin. When the northern kingdom was conquered by Assyria in 722 BCE, those tribes were driven into exile in Khorasan (a region of northern Persia) and thereafter lost to history. In religious and cultural tradition, they are remembered as the "ten lost tribes of Israel." A large number of ethnic and religious groups have claimed to be their descendants. The tribes of Judah and Benjamin (and a few of the landless priests, the Levi), who in 586 BCE were driven from Jerusalem into captivity in Babylon, later returned to reestablish their kingdom and rebuild their temple in Jerusalem. They are believed to be the ancestors of all modern Jews.

fleeing famine, left with his extended family for the fertile soil of the Nile Delta in Egypt, where his descendants, "the children of Israel," remained for many centuries.

Many historians believe that the stories of Jacob's travels are rooted in the early history of the Israelites. These historians agree that some of the Hebrew tribes migrated to Egypt, probably during the mid-17th to the mid-16th centuries BCE. During this period, the Semitic Hyksos kings (probably from Canaan) conquered the northernmost part of Egypt. However, when the Hyksos rulers were deposed in the 16th century BCE, the Hebrews were persecuted and treated as slaves.

Exodus

The children of Israel were led out of captivity in Egypt by a great religious and political leader named Moses. The Old Testament account of their escape details the Ten Plagues that afflicted Egypt, the Passover of the Angel of God that spared first-born Hebrew children, 40 years of wandering the desert, and the handing down at Mount Sinai of God's Ten Commandments (see box, page 122). These events are presented as key elements in the formation of the Israelites' national and religious identity. The date of the Exodus or escape from Egypt is not certain, but many scholars believe that it took place in the 13th century BCE, during the reign of

MOSES AND THE HEBREWS' EXODUS FROM EGYPT

According to the Old Testament books of Exodus and Deuteronomy, Moses—the man who led the Hebrews out of captivity in Egypt—was born to Hebrew parents in Goshen, Egypt. His mother put Moses in a basket made of papyrus and floated it on the river to save him from the pharaoh's order to put all male Hebrew infants to death. The pharaoh's daughter found and raised Moses, and he rose to a position of prominence in the Egyptian government. However, when he saw an Egyptian overseer beat a Hebrew, Moses killed the boorish overseer in a fit of rage and fled into the Sinai Desert to escape retribution. Moses lived there for some time with Semitic nomads and had his first visions of Yahweh, the God of Abraham, Isaac, and Jacob. Yahweh appeared to Moses in a burning bush and commanded him to return to Egypt and lead his people to freedom.

Moses leads the Israelites out of Egypt, while the pursuing Egyptian army is drowned in the Red Sea. The biblical story of the Israelites' journey is probably based on fact.

The pharaoh refused to allow the captive Israelites to leave, so God sent a series of plagues to Egypt. As the last of these plagues, God killed the first-born children in Egypt, saving only those belonging to the Israelites who had marked their doors with lambs' blood. This event is the origin of the Jewish festival of Passover.

Moses, pursued by the pharaoh's army, led the Israelites out from Egypt, God parted the Red Sea to let the Israelites pass and then allowed the waters to break over and drown the Egyptian pursuers. Afterward, the Israelites wandered in the desert for 40 years. This section of the narrative may represent the Israelites' rediscovery of their nomadic and Semitic roots and their gradual abandonment of Egyptian practices.

When the Israelites reached Mount Sinai, Moses communed with God on the mountaintop for a long period, during which God handed down the Ten Commandments. Above all else, the commandments firmly established the concept of monotheism, for they began with the command: "I am the Lord thy God, who has brought you out of the land of Egypt.... You shall have no other gods but me."

Ramses II (1279–1213 BCE) or the reign of his son and successor Merneptah (1213–1204 BCE). By this date, the children of Israel had been in Egypt for around 300 to 400 years.

Moses led his people out of Egypt and through the desert wilderness of northern Egypt and into Jordan. He saw Canaan from the top of Mount Pisgah but died without reaching the Promised Land. Before his death, Moses turned leadership of the people over to a warrior named Joshua. The Israelites remained in what is now Jordan for some years, on the eastern bank of the river of the same name, but in time, they began to cross over into Canaan, the place described to them in Egypt as "a land flowing with milk and honey."

Religious strife

In Canaan, the Israelites encountered Semitic tribes and isolated groups of Hittites, a people who had founded an empire in the region in the 17th century BCE but whose power was now dwindling. According to the biblical account, God had ordered the eradication of the people of Canaan. Some settlers burned towns and villages and slaughtered the inhabitants, but more often than not, this occupation was peaceful—and the native populace was left alone to coexist peacefully with the Israelites.

The Israelites and Canaanites spoke related Semitic languages and were able

This limestone stele carries a depiction of the god Baal. It was found in the city of Ugarit in Canaan.

easily enough to communicate with each other. Religion became a point of conflict, however. It is clear from biblical accounts that the Israelite settlers did not always keep to their tribal faith—the worship of Yahweh, God of Abraham—and were attracted to local pagan cults. The main deities worshipped in Canaan at this time were the rain and fertility god Baal and Ishtar, a goddess of war and sexual love.

Shiloh

The Israelites set up a sanctuary to Yahweh at Shiloh that contained the Ark of the Covenant. Also referred to as the Ark of the Law, the Ark of the Testimony, or the Ark of God, this wooden chest was, according to biblical accounts, 2.5 cubits (3 feet, 9 inches; 1.15 m) long and 1.5 cubits (2 feet, 3 inches; 0.7 m) wide and high. The Israelites took it with them on military campaigns and carried it into battle on poles. The Ark was said to contain both a pot of manna (the food that God sent to feed the Israelites in the desert after their escape from Egypt) and the stone tablets on which the Ten Commandments were carved.

To many Israelites, Yahweh took on the aspects of a god of war. In addition to the sanctuary at Shiloh, the Israelites worshipped Yahweh at Bethel, Gilgal, Mizpah, and Hebron. The Canaanites built sanctuaries to Baal and Ishtar beside the Israelite sanctuaries.

The first king of Israel

For more than a century, the Israelites lived in Canaan without a common leader, but then the Canaanites and Hittites joined forces to combat a new enemy (the Philistines), and the Israelites had to organize themselves as a unified power. The Philistines, one of the Sea Peoples described in Egyptian documents of the period, ransacked towns along the eastern Mediterranean coast. At first, the Philistines occupied only five coastal towns (Gaza, Ashkelon, Ashdod, Ekron, and Gath), but before long, they began to drive the Israelites and the Canaanites farther and farther inland.

The Israelites gradually made the difficult transition from tribal organization under chiefs or judges to the establishment of a single monarchy. The first king of Israel was Saul, who reigned from around 1021 to 1000 BCE. According to biblical accounts, Saul was chosen as king by the seer Samuel and then acclaimed by the people after winning a great victory over the Ammonites. Control of the tribal chiefs had always been limited, and the transition to a strong monarchy was achieved with great difficulty. Saul had to contend with opposition from within his fledgling kingdom as well as from Israel's enemies, but he largely succeeded in his most important task, that of defending Israel. Saul drove the Philistines back toward the coast and defeated the Amalekites, although his reign ended with a defeat at the hands of the resurgent Philistines on the plains of Gilboa.

David and Solomon

Saul's successor, David, expanded the Kingdom of Israel as far as the Red Sea and the Euphrates River. David also established Jerusalem as the capital of the Israelites. This ancient settlement in the arid mountains of Judaea, 35 miles (56 km) east of the Mediterranean and 15 miles (24 km) to the west of the Dead Sea, was founded around 3000 BCE. It was a possession of the Egyptians around 1800 BCE, and in the Amarna Letters, a collection of Egyptian diplomatic correspondence from around 1400 BCE, it was called Uru-Salem (meaning

This 17th-century-CE engraving by Merian Matthäus the Elder depicts the return of the Ark of the Covenant. The Ark was said to contain the stone tablets on which the Ten Commandments were written.

This relief shows the Assyrian king Sennacherib laying siege to the city of Jerusalem.

(Elat) on the eastern arm of the Red Sea, conquered in King David's reign, and traded with Seba (probably southern Arabia). The arrangement enabled Solomon to procure the means to maintain a magnificent court during the highest point of power and importance for ancient Israel and its monarchy.

Israel and Judah under attack

After Solomon's death around 928 BCE, Israel divided into two hostile kingdoms. The main group of the 12 tribes of Israel, fed up with the extravagance of Solomon, rejected the rule of Solomon's son Rehoboam and established the northern Kingdom of Israel, with its capital at Shechem (soon superseded by Samaria) and religious sanctuaries at Dan and Bethel. The tribes of Judah and Benjamin, meanwhile, remained loyal and established the southern Kingdom of Judah, with Jerusalem as its capital and holy city.

Before long, however, Israel and Judah came under attack from the rising powers of Assyria and Babylonia. In 722 BCE, an Assyrian army led by King Sargon II captured Samaria, by then the capital of Israel, and drove thousands of the children of Israel into exile. In 701 BCE, Sennacherib, Sargon's son and successor, led Assyrian armies against the southern Kingdom of Judah. After many brutal victories, Sennacherib besieged Jerusalem but failed to capture it.

The respite for the people of Judah was relatively brief. A little more than a century later, in 586 BCE, Nebuchadnezzar, the king of Babylon, captured Jerusalem, destroying the city and razing the Temple of Solomon to the ground.

"City of Peace"). When David captured the city around 1000 BCE, it was—according to biblical accounts—a stronghold of a Canaanite people called the Jebusites.

David made Jerusalem the center of the Israelite religion. The city consisted of two hills separated by a ravine. Most of the people lived on the western hill, while David established his own royal quarters on the eastern hill, which became known as Zion. David intended to build a great temple and palace, but he died before he could bring the plans to fruition. However, his son King Solomon, using the best Phoenician architects and craftsmen and the finest materials from Lebanon, constructed a superb temple and palace complex in the mid-10th century BCE.

Solomon allied himself with the Phoenician king Hiram of Tyre, who sent a merchant fleet to Ophir (possibly modern Arabia) every three years. Hiram sent sailors and shipbuilders, while Solomon provided the harbor of Ezion-Geber

See also:

The Assyrians (page 102) • Egypt's New Kingdom (page 28) • The Phoenicians (page 90)

THE PERSIANS

The Persian Empire flourished from the late seventh century BCE until the late fourth century BCE. The empire reached the height of its power during the reigns of Cyrus the Great and his successors Cambyses II, Darius I, and Xerxes.

The Persians were originally a nomadic Indo-European people who settled on the Iranian plateau. From the middle of the sixth century BCE, they embarked on a campaign of conquest that enabled them to build an enormous empire, extending from Egypt and Anatolia in the west to northwestern India in the east. It was the largest empire the world had ever known and was to last until 330 BCE, when it fell to the Macedonian king Alexander the Great.

The heartland of this great empire was a vast plateau in southwestern Asia surrounded by volcanic mountain ranges interspersed with some lowlands. Sometime during the third millennium BCE, a hardy people, along with their horses and sheep, spread from the grasslands of central Asia to settle on this plateau between the Persian Gulf and the Caspian Sea. They called themselves Aryans, or Irani, and they called their new homeland Irania (present-day Iran). These people later came to be called Persians because of a mistake made by the Greeks, who named them after the province of Parsa.

The Medes

These Indo-European people gradually abandoned their nomadic lifestyle and settled down as farmers and cattle herders. One group—the Persians— stayed on the plateau; another group— the Indians—moved on to a region on the Indian subcontinent between the Indus and Ganges rivers. Around 700 BCE, a number of tribes on the plateau attempted to form a kingdom. These people were the Medes. According to the Greek historian Herodotus, the first Median king was Deioces. Although the accuracy of this account is not certain, it seems that Deioces established a capital for the new kingdom at Ekbatana (present-day Hamadan).

A later Median king, Phraortes, ruled from around 675 to 653 BCE. Leading an army of Median tribes, all carrying only a long spear and a wicker shield, Phraortes braved the might of the Assyrians, meeting them in a battle in 653 BCE. However, the Medes were defeated and Phraortes was slain. He was succeeded by his son Cyaxares, who modernized the army and added bows and arrows to its arsenal of weapons. Cyaxares succeeded in banishing a northern nomadic people known as the Scythians, who had invaded Median territory in his father's reign, and in 612 BCE, with the help of the Babylonians, Cyaxares captured Nineveh, the Assyrian capital. The city was thoroughly destroyed and never rebuilt. The loss of Nineveh marked the beginning of the downfall of the Assyrian Empire.

Cyrus the Great

The last Median king was Astyages, son of Cyaxares. Astyages inherited a large kingdom from his father, including the vassal kingdoms of the Persians. Despite his long reign from 585 to 550 BCE, Astyages, preferring a life of luxury, did little to consolidate his empire. He did, however, marry his daughter to the Persian king, Cambyses I. In 559 BCE, that couple's son became the Persian vassal king Cyrus II.

Cyrus II was descended from the Persian king Achaemenes, and for this reason, the Persian dynasty he was to found was called the Achaemenids. Cyrus was ambitious to restore the fortunes of the Persians, and soon after he became king, he united several Persian and Iranian tribes and led a revolt against Astyages. An army with Astyages at its head set out to quell the rebellion, but when the army

This relief from around the sixth century BCE depicts two sphinxes, animals that are commonly seen in art from the Persian Empire.

reached the capital of Parsa, the generals mutinied and handed Astyages over to Cyrus. In 550 BCE, the triumphant Persians captured Ekbatana and seized its treasury of gold and silver.

The Persians under Cyrus had routed the Medes, and the vanquished Median Empire now became the Persian Empire. However, the Persians did not wreak vengeance upon the Median people. Under Persian rule, Medes were often appointed to high official positions and even given commands in the Persian army.

Conquest of Lydia

In the far west of Anatolia, King Croesus of Lydia heard of the fall of the Median Empire and took the opportunity to invade former Median territory with the hope of extending his own kingdom. Legend has it that Croesus consulted the oracle at Delphi in Greece before setting out on his campaign. In answer to his question about whether it was wise to go to war, Croesus was told that if he crossed the Halys River (the border with the former Median Empire) to engage with the Persians, an empire would fall. Unfortunately, he did not realize that the doomed empire was his own.

Eager to defend the borders of his new empire (and probably eager also to capture Croesus's immense treasury of gold), Cyrus drove Croesus back across the Halys River and pushed on into Lydia. On a small plain near the Lydian capital of Sardis, Cyrus's army was confronted by a troop of Lydian cavalry armed with spears. Taking the advice of his general, Cyrus brought to the front the camels that were carrying the army's baggage. The enemy horses took fright at the camels' horrible smell, turned tail, and bolted. Cyrus forced the remnants of the Lydian army back into Sardis and then laid siege to the city. After two weeks, his engineers succeeded in scaling

the walls. The city was taken, and Croesus was captured. Cyrus put Croesus to death and annexed Lydia and the Greek coastal cities of Ionia that had previously been subject to Lydia.

Turning east, Cyrus set his sights on Babylon. A successful campaign through the Iranian lands had not only doubled the size of his empire but also swelled the ranks of his army with soldiers drawn from the defeated regions. His march on Babylon was largely unopposed, since the country was suffering from the weak rule of the scholarly King Nabonidus. Famine threatened the peasants, and the population was looking for someone to deliver it from its predicament. Cyrus reached Babylon in October of 539 BCE and took the city without a battle.

Cyrus was in possession of the whole Babylonian Empire, which included Syria and Palestine. He proved himself to be a benevolent ruler and was soon popular with the Babylonians. He rebuilt the ruined temples and restored statues of the gods (which had been removed by Nabonidus) to their rightful places. Cyrus also decreed that the Jews, who had been exiled to Babylon from Palestine, were free to return home and that the temple in Jerusalem (which had been destroyed by the Babylonian kings) should be rebuilt and its gold and silver utensils should be restored.

Cyrus established his capital city at Pasargadae, in the southern part of Iran. His palace there was set in a park and contained a great hall fronted by an impressive porch consisting of two rows of 20 wooden columns, each 20 feet (6 m) high. The park later contained his tomb, which was constructed from huge blocks of white limestone and bore the inscription "Here I lie, Cyrus, king of kings." The last years of Cyrus's reign were spent defending his eastern frontier, where he was killed in battle in 529 BCE.

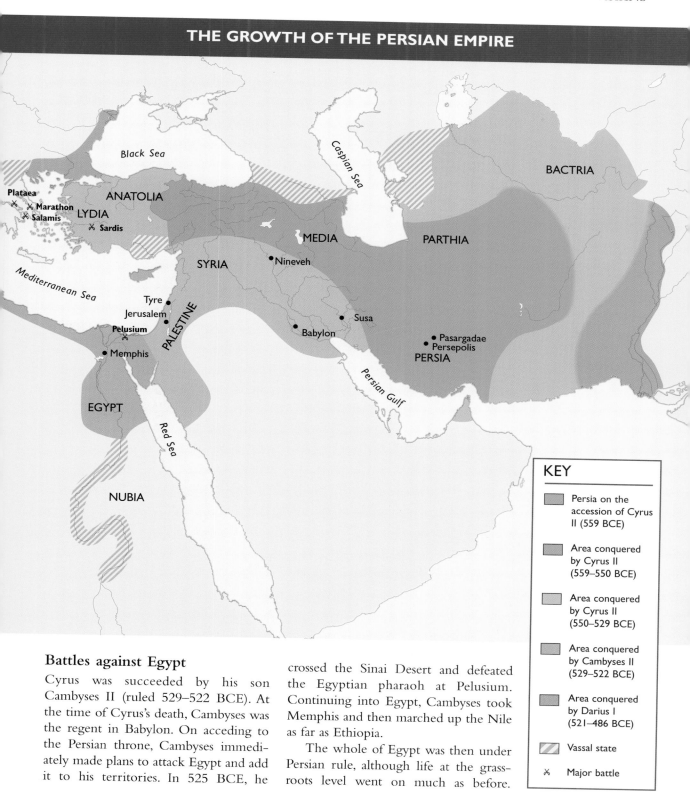

THE GROWTH OF THE PERSIAN EMPIRE

Black Sea

BACTRIA

Caspian Sea

Plataea
✕ ✕ **Marathon**
ANATOLIA
✕ **Salamis**
LYDIA
✕ **Sardis**

MEDIA

PARTHIA

SYRIA

● **Nineveh**

Mediterranean Sea

Tyre ●
Jerusalem ●
PALESTINE
Pelusium ✕
● **Babylon**
● **Susa**

● **Pasargadae**
Persepolis
PERSIA

● **Memphis**

Persian Gulf

EGYPT

Red Sea

NUBIA

KEY

⬛	Persia on the accession of Cyrus II (559 BCE)
⬛	Area conquered by Cyrus II (559–550 BCE)
⬛	Area conquered by Cyrus II (550–529 BCE)
⬛	Area conquered by Cambyses II (529–522 BCE)
⬛	Area conquered by Darius I (521–486 BCE)
▨	Vassal state
✕	Major battle

Battles against Egypt

Cyrus was succeeded by his son Cambyses II (ruled 529–522 BCE). At the time of Cyrus's death, Cambyses was the regent in Babylon. On acceding to the Persian throne, Cambyses immediately made plans to attack Egypt and add it to his territories. In 525 BCE, he crossed the Sinai Desert and defeated the Egyptian pharaoh at Pelusium. Continuing into Egypt, Cambyses took Memphis and then marched up the Nile as far as Ethiopia.

The whole of Egypt was then under Persian rule, although life at the grass-roots level went on much as before.

Cambyses honored the Egyptian gods and restored their temples, although he did substantially reduce the revenues allotted to the temples. This reduction of the temple revenues may have earned Cambyses his reputation as a harsh ruler.

In 522 BCE, Cambyses learned that his brother Bardiya had seized control of the empire. Cambyses hastily set out back to Persia to quell this revolt, but he died on the way. It was left to a young prince of the Achaemenid line, Darius, to put down the rebellion and claim the empire for himself.

The reign of Darius I

At the beginning of 522 BCE, Darius (ruled 521–486 BCE) was 28 years of age and, according to the Greek historian Herodotus, one of the king's spear-bearers in Egypt. It seems likely that as soon as Cambyses died, Darius left the army and hastened back to Media to join with a party of nobles to usurp the usurper.

The palace of Cyrus the Great at Pasargadae. Pasargadae was the first capital of the Persian Empire.

After almost two years of civil strife all over the empire, Darius finally succeeded in quelling all opposition and took the Persian throne as Darius I. On the Behistun Inscription (see box, page 137) Darius claimed his right to rule through his descent from princes of the royal blood. Darius also claimed that Cambyses had slain Bardiya before going to Egypt and that it was an imposter, Gaumatan, who had rebelled in Bardiya's name.

The first imperative for Darius on ascending the throne was to restore order in a war-torn empire. Darius was an able administrator, and he set about restoring and strengthening the system of satrapies (provinces) that had been instituted by Cyrus II. The empire was divided into 20 satrapies, each a vast territory ruled over by a satrap (governor) who was directly responsible to the king. Each province also had a military commander who took instructions directly from the king, thereby ensuring military supervision of the whole empire. In addition,

This frieze shows how soldiers would have dressed during the reign of Darius I. The frieze originally adorned the walls of the king's palace.

THE PERSIAN ARMY

The Persian army of the sixth and fifth centuries BCE was, at that time, the most massive army that had ever existed. At one point in time, the army is said to have comprised more than a million soldiers, although such claims are probably exaggerated. All subjugated people had to supply troops to Persia, which resulted in an army that consisted of groups of foreign soldiers who each had trained to fight with different weapons and with different strategies.

The king had three units of royal troops, each consisting of 2,000 horsemen and 2,000 infantry, and an elite regiment of 10,000 soldiers called the Immortals. These Immortals were the king's personal bodyguard, and their number never fell below 10,000; there was always a replacement ready to step into the shoes of any Immortal who became ill or died. The uniform of the Immortals was richly decorated with gold, and each soldier carried a spear, a bow, and a quiver of arrows. The members of this privileged regiment were allowed to take servants and concubines along on campaigns.

The provinces all had to supply their own contingents of troops, which were divided into squads, companies, regiments, and brigades that consisted of ten, one hundred, one thousand, and ten thousand troops respectively. Altogether, the army of Xerxes had six corps, each under its own corps commander. Many of the provinces also supplied cavalry and charioteers, while the maritime provinces supplied ships and oarsmen for the redoubtable Persian navy. The Persian army on the move was a truly formidable sight, calculated to inspire terror in the hearts of all who saw it.

131

Darius established a secret service, called "the king's eyes and ears," which consisted of messengers who inspected each province annually and reported back to the king.

Darius also instituted a new legal system to be imposed on the whole empire. In each province, there were to be two courts. One court would hear cases relating to local laws. The other court would deal with cases that came under Persian imperial jurisdiction. The tax system was also revised by Darius. While Persians were only required to pay taxes in times of national emergency, each province had to pay a fixed annual amount of money and goods to the king's treasury. Because of the different harvest sizes in the various provinces, surveyors were sent out to estimate the yield in each province, and taxes were assessed accordingly. Another improvement carried out by Darius was to establish a uniform system of coinage throughout the empire, which, together with standardized weights and measures, greatly simplified the process of collecting taxes.

Territorial expansion

With his empire more or less under control, Darius turned his attention to further expansion. A campaign to the east secured new territories right up to the Indus River. Another campaign in 516 BCE against the Scythians north of the Black Sea was not so successful, and Darius was forced to withdraw. A rebellion by the Greek cities in Ionia in 500 BCE had to be suppressed, and after that, Darius set his sights on the Greek mainland. At first, Darius met with some success. However, he was thoroughly defeated at the Battle of Marathon in 490 BCE. A revolt in Egypt followed, but just as Darius was preparing to move

The tomb of the Persian king Cyrus the Great is located in Pasargadae (in southern Iran), which was the location of Cyrus's palace when he was alive.

to quell the latest rebellion, he died at the age of 64, leaving his son and successor, Xerxes, to crush the Egyptians.

Xerxes

In contrast to his predecessor, Xerxes (ruled 486–465 BCE) proved himself to be a heavy-handed ruler of Egypt. Ignoring the usual forms of Egyptian rule, he imposed Persian law, riding roughshod over local sensibilities. Xerxes proved equally ruthless when the Babylonians rebelled against Persian rule in 482 BCE. After the city of Babylon was retaken, the fortifications and ziggu-

This relief sculpture of an unidentified man was found at Persepolis and dates to the reign of Darius I.

rat were demolished, together with many other temples. The golden statue of the god Marduk was removed and melted down, while all the citizens of Babylon saw their possessions confiscated and handed over to the Persians. The policies of Xerxes were in complete contrast to those of earlier Persian kings, who had been tolerant of local gods and religions and who had even rebuilt the local temples on occasion.

In 480 BCE, Xerxes invaded Greece with an army of 70,000 men. At first, the campaign went well, and Athens was captured. However, in a great sea battle at Salamis, the Persians were defeated and lost a third of their fleet. When the Persians were subsequently beaten, this time on land, at the Battle of Plataea in 479 BCE, the campaign petered out, and Xerxes lost interest in any further attempts to expand his empire.

After Xerxes was assassinated in 465 BCE, a century of rebellion and civil war ensued. Various members of the Achaemenid royal house at times gained power and at others plotted against each other. During this period, the empire inevitably suffered; it was never again to know the firm direction it had enjoyed under Darius. Despite its military weakness, Persia did play a significant diplomatic role in the Peloponnesian Wars, which involved Athens and Sparta. Persia supplied first one side and then the other with financial aid in return for political concessions.

The coming of Alexander

When Darius III succeeded to the throne in 336 BCE, he found himself under threat from the might of Alexander the Great of Macedonia, who had already conquered Greece and was eager to extend his empire. Alexander marched on Persia, winning three battles before capturing the capital, Persepolis, in 330 BCE. In triumph, Alexander held

PERSEPOLIS

Work on the great city of Persepolis was started by Darius I and completed by his son Xerxes. Darius intended the city to be the capital of the Persian Empire, reflecting both its might and wealth. He also wanted a luxurious royal residence fit for an all-powerful king. Darius chose a site a few miles southwest of Pasargadae, the old capital of Cyrus the Great. Work started on the fortifications sometime around 500 BCE. A great perimeter wall was constructed on a natural platform at the base of the Mount of Mercy. The wall consisted of huge limestone blocks topped by mud bricks, bringing the total height in places to 60 feet (18.2 m).

The royal palace was situated on the west side of the citadel. The palace included a large reception hall, called the Apadana, which featured imposing columns of stone up to 65 feet (20 m) high. The columns were topped with ornate capitals

The remains of the palace of Darius at Persepolis. Much of the palace was destroyed by fire on the orders of Alexander the Great.

supporting the timber beams that held up the roof. South of the Apadana were the many private royal apartments, including a harem.

The palace housed many ceremonial gates and stairways, all decorated with elaborate stone carvings, which were carried out by an army of stone carvers, wood carvers, goldsmiths, silversmiths, and other artists. Almost every stone surface carried a carved relief. These magnificent examples of Persian art are nowhere seen to better effect than in the Apadana, where there were scenes of palms and cypresses, lions and bulls, culminating in the depiction of a great procession of nobles, courtiers, soldiers, and representatives of the subject peoples advancing to greet their king.

On the east side of the citadel, Xerxes built a vast throne room that had 10 rows of columns with 10 columns in each row, giving rise to its modern name, the Hall of a Hundred Columns. The hall was entered through a porch on the north side. The porch was held up by 16

columns, each decorated at the top by a bull with a human head. The eight doorways into the hall were all decorated with reliefs.

This palace complex was sacked by Alexander the Great in 330 BCE, and the buildings were put to the torch. According to some sources, Alexander's order to burn the palace was given while he was drunk at a feast and being urged on by his fellow revelers.

The remains of the city of Persepolis, which was the capital of the Persian Empire. The city was famous throughout the ancient world for its riches.

a great feast in the palace at Persepolis—and the next morning burned it to the ground. Persepolis itself—reputedly the richest city under the sun—was looted of its treasures, all the men were put to the sword, and the women were enslaved. In the same year that Persepolis was taken, Darius was murdered, probably by his own followers, and the history of the Persian Empire was at an end.

Religion

The early Persians worshipped a variety of gods, many of whom were associated with natural phenomena, such as the sun. However, around 600 BCE, a great prophet started expounding the tenets of a new religion that recognized just one god, called Ahura Mazda (Lord of Wisdom). The prophet's name was Zoroaster (or Zarathustra), and the religion he preached was eventually to become the official religion of the Persian Empire.

Zoroaster is believed to have lived for around 77 years. The stories told about him testify to his desire to help the poor and unfortunate. In his youth, during a period of great drought, he is said to have distributed his father's stores of food to the poor. On another occasion, he tried to save a half-starved dog and its five pups. When he was 20, he left his parents' house and embarked on a search for the most just and merciful person he could find. He traveled for seven years, and during that time, he began to formulate the ideas behind his new religion.

135

Zoroaster rejected all but one of the many gods of his day. He chose to worship Ahura Mazda as the one all-powerful god, the embodiment of good. Ahura Mazda's adversary was Angra Mainyu, the personification of evil. The world was created, said Zoroaster, in the struggle between the two of them. Since then, the conflict between good and evil, light and dark, has been a never-ending battle.

This bronze harness ring, discovered in the Luristan region of western Iran, was made between the 10th and 7th centuries BCE.

The prophet struggled for many years to persuade people to relinquish their beliefs in the old magic cults and adhere to his new faith. Even though he was not very eloquent, he was determined to free his people from the grip of irrational superstition. "As a priest," he is recorded as saying, "I will continue to search for the paths of righteousness and teach the way to cultivate the earth." It seems he was persecuted for his teachings, and he writes: "To which country shall I flee? Where shall I hide?" For a moment, his faith seems to waver: "Do not desert me Ahura Mazda. Help me as a friend who helps his friends. Teach me to think well and correctly."

Evidently, his prayers were answered. After ten years of preaching, Zoroaster made his first convert—his cousin Maidioman, who became his disciple. Two years later, a local king called Hystaspes also converted and embraced the new religion very enthusiastically. Hystaspes and Zoroaster became close friends, and the king converted his entire court to the new religion. Hystaspes also undertook military campaigns with the aim of imposing the teachings of Zoroaster on neighboring peoples.

Hystaspes was probably only a minor ruler who had to pay tribute to the nomadic Tartars who were his neighbors. Urged on by his new belief and by the prophet, Hystaspes waged two successful holy wars against the Tartars to end this humiliating situation. The triumphs of Hystaspes greatly enhanced the reputation of the faith among the Persian people.

It is believed that Zoroaster was murdered around 550 BCE by fanatic Tartars or by a hostile religious figure defending the old faith. In some legends, the prophet's death is depicted as a supernatural event; he is said to have been carried off to heaven by a flash of lightning to save him from cruel tortures.

The Avesta

Zoroaster's teachings are preserved in the Avesta, the sacred books of Zoroastrianism. The Avesta was compiled around 224 CE and is based on the writings of Zoroaster himself. In it, he preaches a faith in a benevolent god, Ahura Mazda, and describes the eternal conflict between good and evil. The good spirit battles its opposite spirit, which has chosen evil. The first spirit works toward unity and creativity, while the second only seeks to destroy. Human beings, says the prophet, must chose between the two. If they opt for the side of good, they support Ahura Mazda in his work. Ahura Mazda demands right thinking, honesty, devotion, and health (all manifestations of good) from his followers. In his youth, Zoroaster was influenced by the cult of fire, which maintained that all evil on earth would eventually be purified by fire.

According to the writings in the Avesta, the supreme god Ahura Mazda created 16 countries, the first of which was Airyana Vaeja, the cradle of all people. Although described as an area with many good features, this country was endowed with winter and serpents by the evil force, Angra Mainyu. The winter (which was considered to be "the worst of horrors" by Ahura Mazda) lasted for 10 months, while the summer lasted for only 2 months. This duality pervaded the religion. For every good creation of Ahura Mazda, his enemy Angra Mainyu counters with a disaster.

Early migration

After describing the 15 other countries, the Avesta retells a legend linked to the emigration of the early Indo-Europeans from Persia. Yima, the first Indo-European king of a tribal people, takes it upon himself "to extend the country," which is packed with herds, people, and dogs. After leading three attempts to emigrate, Yima goes south toward the sun and touches the earth with his dagger and his seal ring, ordering the earth to expand to twice its size: "Open, earth, and extend yourself in order to feed more people and animals."

According to the Avesta, dogs and cattle were the only domestic animals kept by the Persians as they migrated. Persians held dogs in high esteem and considered them only slightly less developed than humans—the punishment for

THE BEHISTUN INSCRIPTION

One of the most important sources of information about the reign of the Persian king Darius I is an inscription on a rock face in the foothills of the Zagros Mountains. The text is known as the Behistun Inscription, from the ancient name of the nearby town of Bisitun. The location of the inscription is extremely inaccessible.

The inscription lists Darius's ancestors, details his rise to power and his defeat of the imposter Gaumata (who had rebelled in Bardiya's name), and gives accounts of Darius's many victories over peoples such as the Babylonians, the Medes, and the Elamites. The text is accompanied by a life-size carving of Darius standing with his foot on Gaumata's chest.

The Behistun Inscription is important for more than just its content. The text is written three times, once in Old Persian, once in Elamite, and once in Babylonian. The fact that the text was the same in all three cases allowed linguists to translate these languages for the first time.

The first person in modern times to attempt to translate the inscription was Sir Henry Rawlinson, a British soldier and academic who began work on the Old Persian inscription in 1835. He managed a complete translation of the text by 1838. Five years later, Rawlinson returned to Bisitun to copy the other two inscriptions, which were gradually translated during the following years.

Lifestyle

Herodotus also provided a description of the Persians' lifestyle, saying that they had no statues of gods, or temples, or altars (although archaeological evidence says otherwise). "They also bring offerings to the god of the sun, the moon, fire, water, and wind," he continues. "Of all the feasts, the most important one for the Persians is their birthday." He goes on to say that after courage, the Persians most admire fertility: "Each year the king sends gifts to the family with the most children." According to Herodotus, children were taught only three things between the ages of 5 and 20—horseback riding, archery, and telling the truth. "The most contemptuous deed is to tell a lie," Herodotus reports, "and after that comes getting into debt. The Persians never pollute the waters of their rivers with garbage, and neither do they wash their hands in them. They consider the rivers to be holy."

Before the rise of their empire, the Persians were still a relatively primitive people. When Croesus of Lydia was preparing to go to war with the Persians around 550 BCE, one of his counselors advised him: "You are going to war against a people who wear leather pants, live off dry ground, drink water rather than wine, and do not know figs. If you conquer them, you will still own nothing. If they vanquish you they will be incredibly rich."

Whatever their reputation, the Persian lifestyle certainly did not exclude a love of wine. The alcoholic tendencies of Cambyses II were legendary, and Herodotus reports of the Persians: "It is their custom to discuss business when they are drunk—but they only make their decisions the next day, when they are sober again."

Despite this dubious press, the Persian kings were on the whole enlightened and benevolent rulers. For the most part,

Ahura Mazda was the chief god of the Zoroastrian religion. Rituals involving the worship of Ahura Mazda were often performed at outdoor altars. This altar is located in southwestern Iran.

the ill-treatment of dogs and slaves was the same. The Avesta advises owners to feed dogs milk and meat and to punish the dogs as if they were responsible for their behavior. After the first attack by a dog, its right ear was to be cut off; after the second, its left ear; and so on.

Most of the Persian priests belonged to the Median tribe and were called Magi. The Magi adapted many of Zoroaster's teachings and used them for their own purposes. In the Avesta, fragments of Zoroaster's original teachings are found mingled with age-old tales about the evil spirits of the steppes and detailed descriptions of magicians' rites. The Greek historian Herodotus considered many of the Persian rituals to be of Magi origin, including the protection of dogs and the funeral practice of leaving corpses to be destroyed by the elements rather than burying or cremating them.

when they conquered a territory, they respected the local customs and gods and often employed local people as officials. Although the regional satrapies had to pay heavy taxes, in return they enjoyed the benefits of the public projects that the Persian government carried out throughout the empire. These projects included improving drainage and irrigation of agricultural land by constructing a system of underground channels to carry water in desert regions. One vast water project carried out during Darius's reign was the building of a great canal to link the Red Sea with the Mediterranean Sea. The journey along the canal took four days to complete.

The Royal Road

The Persians built a great network of roads that made traveling from one part of the empire to another relatively simple. The greatest one of these roads,

which was called the Royal Road, covered a distance of 1,550 miles (2,500 km) and linked Sardis in Lydia to the one-time Persian capital of Susa. There were staging posts along all the main routes where travelers could change horses, get a meal, and take some rest. This road network enabled messengers for the king to travel at great speed, keeping him informed of events in even the most remote parts of his empire. The network also enabled relays of messengers on horseback to provide a fast, efficient postal service. Herodotus was so impressed by these messengers that he wrote of them, "Neither snow, nor rain, nor heat, nor gloom of night stays these couriers from the swift completion of their appointed rounds."

See also:

The Assyrians (page 102) • The Babylonians (page 62)

This statue of a griffin is located at Persepolis, the capital of the Persian Empire.

GLOSSARY

Ahura Mazda Zoroastrian god of light and truth.

Akhetaton city built by the Egyptian pharaoh Akhenaton to replace the old Egyptian capital at Thebes; modern Amarna, Egypt.

Akkadians Semitic people who flourished in the third millennium BCE; named after Akkad, the capital of their empire.

Amarna Letters archive of clay tablets written in Babylonian cuneiform script; found at Akhetaton.

Amorites Semitic people who invaded Mesopotamia from the north and northwest beginning around 2000 BCE.

Anubis ancient Egyptian god of the dead; depicted as a jackal or as a man with the head of a jackal.

Aramaeans Semitic people who invaded southern Mesopotamia around 1100 BCE.

Aryans prehistoric inhabitants of Iran and northern India.

Assyrians people of northern Mesopotamia whose independent state, established in the 14th century BCE, became a major power in the region.

ba in ancient Egyptian religion, one of the three main aspects of the soul, along with ka (the sum of a person's physical and intellectual qualities) and akh (the spirit in the hereafter).

Babylon major city in southern Mesopotamia. From 612 to 539 BCE, Babylon was the capital of the Neo-Babylonian Empire.

bronze copper-tin alloy widely used by 1700 BCE.

Bronze Age period during which bronze became the most important basic material; began around 3500 BCE in western Asia and around 1900 BCE in Europe.

Canaanites Semitic tribes who settled in Palestine and the western Levant in the third millennium BCE and mixed with the native population. They maintained separate city-states. Around 1200 BCE, their territory was infiltrated by Israelites and Philistines.

cartouche oval frame enclosing the hieroglyphs of the name of an Egyptian sovereign.

Chaldeans Aramaean people from southern Mesopotamia who caused the fall of Assyria in the seventh century BCE.

cuneiform writing system with wedge-shaped characters that emerged at the end of the fourth millennium BCE. Cuneiform writing was used by the Sumerians and other early civilizations of western Asia.

Damascus ancient capital of a city-state in Roman times; conquered variously by David of Israel, Assyrian Tiglath-pileser III in 732 BCE, and Alexander the Great in 333–332 BCE; part of the Seleucid kingdom until taken by Pompey the Great in 64 BCE. Made a Christian bishopric in the first century CE, it was taken over by Muslims in 635 CE and by Turks in 1056 CE. Damascus was besieged by the Christians in 1148 CE. In 1154 CE, it fell to the Egyptians. It was the headquarters of Saladin during the Third Crusade.

Early Dynastic period era of Egyptian history, also known as the Archaic period, when the pharaohs developed an effective system of ruling the whole of Egypt; lasted from around 2925 to 2650 BCE.

Elam ancient country in western Asia, roughly equivalent to modern southwestern Iran.

ensi governor of a Sumerian city-state; temple king and ruler of the city on behalf of the deity and the temple.

Epic of Gilgamesh ancient poem written in the Akkadian language. The earliest surviving written version was inscribed in cuneiform script in the seventh century BCE.

Euphrates river of western Asia that flows from the mountains of western Asia to the Persian Gulf. Its lower reaches form the western edge of Mesopotamia.

Gutians Iranian mountain people who invaded the Akkadian Empire repeatedly between around 2230 and 2100 BCE.

Heliopolis city of ancient Egypt and site of a great temple to the sun god Re.

hieroglyphics writing system found in inscriptions on Egyptian monuments that uses characters in the form of pictures.

Hittites people who established an empire in western Asia around 2000 BCE and were the first to base their power on iron processing. Their civilization peaked around 1500 BCE.

Horus Egyptian sun god and son of Osiris; represented as a falcon.

Hurrians tribe from the east that settled in northern Mesopotamia around 1800 BCE. They founded the Mitanni Empire ruled by a militarily superior Indo-European elite. After 1200 BCE, the Hurrians settled in Urartu and from there conquered parts of Syria and Phoenicia.

Hyksos Asiatic people who settled in Egypt during the 17th century BCE. They later ruled the kingdom.

Inanna Sumerian fertility goddess; daughter of Anu (the god of heaven and ruler of the gods).

Indo-European languages common family of European and Asiatic (Indian) languages.

iron metallic element that can be made into tools, weapons, and ornaments. Iron was being processed in western Asia by 3000 BCE.

Iron Age period during which major tools and weapons were made of iron; followed the Bronze Age. The Hittites formed the first Iron Age culture around 1700 BCE.

Ishtar Semitic war goddess who merged with Inanna and became the goddess of love and fertility.

Israelites Semitic tribes who infiltrated Canaan in the second millennium BCE. They probably stayed in Egypt or in the border area between around 1650 and 1214 BCE. After 1200 BCE, they conquered Canaan, according to the Bible. They lived in a loose alliance of tribes but joined under a king around 1000 BCE.

Kush kingdom of southern Egypt; part of modern Sudan. In the Late period, the Kushites ruled Egypt.

Lagash Sumerian city-state that constituted a dominant empire in Mesopotamia in the 22nd century BCE.

Late period era, from around 671 BCE, when Egypt was ruled by a succession of foreign powers: the Kushites, the Assyrians, the Persians, and finally, in 332 BCE, the Greeks under Alexander the Great.

lugal political leader in the Sumerian city-states.

Medes Indo-European people who entered northeastern Iran around the 17th century BCE.

Memphis city in Lower (northern) Egypt; residence of the pharaohs during the Old Kingdom and during the time of the Ramesside kings.

Mesopotamia area in western Asia between the Euphrates and Tigris rivers; location of several of the world's first great civilizations, including that of Sumer.

Middle Kingdom period of Egyptian history, from around 2150 to 1550 BCE, during which unity was restored by the Theban kings.

Mitanni Hurrian kingdom that flourished in northern Mesopotamia from around 1500 to 1350 BCE.

mummification method of preserving human remains by embalming.

New Kingdom period of Egyptian history that lasted from around 1550 to 1075 BCE.

Nile world's longest river; flows north from central Africa into Egypt. All of the great cities of ancient Egypt grew up on its banks.

Nineveh city of the ancient Assyrian Empire; situated on the east bank of the Tigris River opposite modern Mosul (Iraq).

Nubia region in Africa, extending approximately from the Nile River Valley to the shores of the Red Sea, southward to Khartoum, and westward to the Libyan Desert.

Old Kingdom period of Egyptian history that lasted from around 2650 to 2150 BCE.

Osiris ancient Egyptian god of death and the underworld.

Persepolis important center of the Persian kingdom of the Achaemenids. From the reign of Darius, it was also a major royal citadel with multicolumned halls. Persepolis was destroyed by Alexander the Great.

pharaoh Egyptian king, who also acted as legislator, military general, and religious leader. Later, he was considered the son of Re.

Phoenicia ancient region roughly corresponding to modern Lebanon. Its inhabitants, the Phoenicians, were merchants, traders, and colonizers of the Mediterranean region in the first millennium BCE.

pyramid Egyptian royal tomb with triangular sides and a square base. Pyramid construction reached its height between around 2600 and 2400 BCE.

Re Egyptian sun god. The pharaoh was considered his son and ascended to his heavenly empire after death.

relief figurative sculpture that projects from a supporting background, which is usually a plane surface.

Scythians nomadic people who migrated from central Asia to the northern coast of the Black Sea in the eighth and seventh centuries BCE.

Sea Peoples maritime warriors of uncertain origin who invaded Egypt and other coastal regions of the eastern Mediterranean Sea at the end of the Bronze Age.

Semites people residing in northern and southern Mesopotamia. They spoke a different language from the Sumerians and largely dwelt in rural areas. They founded the Akkadian Empire around 2335 BCE.

Sidon city on the Phoenician coast that was a powerful trading center (c. 1400–700 BCE). Phoenicians were often called Sidonians.

stele standing stone slab used in the ancient world either to mark the site of a grave or to commemorate a historic event.

Sumerians people of Sumer, in Mesopotamia, the site of the earliest known civilization, which emerged around 3400 BCE.

Tigris great river of western Asia that flows from the mountains of eastern Turkey to the Persian Gulf. Its lower reaches form the eastern edge of Mesopotamia.

Tyre Phoenician city situated on an island off the coast of Lebanon. Tyre was a booming trade city from the 10th century BCE and founded many colonies, including Carthage.

Ugarit trading town in northern Canaan; Semitic city-state from the third millennium BCE. After reaching its height of power (c. 1550–1360 BCE), Ugarit was controlled by the Hittites. It was destroyed by the Sea Peoples around 1200 BCE.

Ur Sumerian city-state that constituted a centralized empire in Mesopotamia from around 2100 to 2000 BCE.

Uruk Sumerian city-state in Mesopotamia to the northwest of Ur. The ancient site was first excavated in 1928 CE.

Valley of the Kings area on the western bank of the Nile River opposite Thebes. New Kingdom pharaohs were buried there.

vizier high Egyptian administrative official; usually a close relative of the pharaoh.

ziggurat pyramidal, stepped temple towers built from brick in Mesopotamia between around 2200 and 500 BCE.

INDEX